Through the Glass Ceiling

Through the Glass Ceiling

Christine E King
BA, MA, PhD, FIM, FRHistS

First published in Great Britain by Tudor Business Publishing Limited. Sole distributors worldwide, Hodder and Stoughton (Publishers) Ltd, Mill Road, Dunton Green, Sevenoaks, Kent, TN13 2XX.

British Library Cataloging in Publication Data

King, Christine
   Through the Glass Ceiling: Effective
   Senior Management Development for Women
   I. Title
   658.40082

Typeset by Deltatype Ltd, Ellesmere Port, Cheshire
Printed and bound by Athenaeum Press Ltd, Newcastle upon Tyne.

Contents

Introduction   1

1 A Woman's Way?   9
2 Women and Meetings   23
3 Women and Men Working together   36
4 Women Working with Women   51
5 How do I Manage the Boundaries?   67
6 Is It All Worth It?   83
7 The Next Step: How to Take It   106
Conclusion   121
Bibliography   129
Addresses   132

Introduction

Women are increasingly aware of the 'glass ceiling' which, whilst invisible from above, is a real barrier preventing their progress into more responsible and senior positions in a variety of careers. Some are identifying a backlash against the progress women appeared to make during the 70s and 80s and more than one source is urging women not to 'rock the boat' by stressing their differences and the obstacles they face.

Nevertheless, however they play it, women in the UK are losing out. They earn, on average, just 77% of men's hourly earnings and their representation in top management is barely statistically visible. The Equal Opportunities Commission argues that only 4% of important middle management posts are held by women and fewer than 2% of senior executive posts.

The UK is perhaps behind the rest of Europe and certainly behind the USA, where there are affirmative action programmes for women. The Social Chapter of the Maastricht Treaty, which the British government alone of the twelve has so far refused to sign, proposes directives on workers' rights that would benefit five million UK women.

A report from the Institute of Management reveals that women managers and professionals in the UK see the strongest barrier they face as coming from the operation of an 'old boys' network'. Women in the public sector are faring as badly as their counterparts in industry and are simply not being promoted, even when applying on the same terms as men.

As the recession has its impact and the forces of orthodoxy and conservatism assert themselves, so, paradoxically, many companies are identifying as key management characteristics those skills and strengths which many people, the authors of this book included, would say are often found in women leaders and managers. Tomorrow's managers, it is argued, will need different skills to cope with the new patterns of life and work which are emerging in the context of techno-logical and demographic trends. They will need to be flexible and adaptable and to be what Charles Handy calls 'post-heroic' leaders, able to delegate and enthuse others.

By the year 2000, women will provide 45% of the work force. More and more women are turning already to start their own businesses and it looks like this trend will continue. Women are in some critical middle management roles already. If this trend continues, and good practice from parts of Europe and the USA spreads, then women's style, certainly at middle management levels, should become far less exceptional and far more the norm. The advice which women often receive to play it 'like one of the boys' will have less currency.

The debate about women's style and women's opportunities is now global. The late 80s saw a boom in the economy and a demonstrable growth in women's opportunities in Japan. Some companies were planning to introduce a special fast track for women when the bubble burst as women who joined companies for the first time found that the old values quickly reasserted themselves and they were excluded from policy making roles and from promotion opportunities. In France, the status of women over the last two decades has changed slowly for the better. Europe as a whole saw, in the 70s, the introduction of a range of anti-discriminatory legislation and a woman's right to equal pay for equal work was established in principle, even if the practice still slips. The result has meant women's entry to many professions, but across the continent they find themselves stuck at a middle management level, without the means to move onwards and upwards.

There are schemes run by the European Community to encourage training and the exchange of ideas across Europe and these are based on the premise that not only do women need training and opportunities, but that the culture of many companies and organisations has to change. The news from eastern Europe worries many women in the west. There are cuts in those very public service industries where women traditionally work and the political and economic problems mean that women's choices are severely limited.

Women managers everywhere seem, on the whole, to pay a high price for career advancement. They are statistically less likely than their male counterparts to be married and those who are, are also much less likely to have children. Where they do have children, this fact has a noticeable impact on their careers and the famous 'career-break' means that returners are less likely to reach the top. UK firms have not adopted the 'mummy-track' route debated in America, where young mothers would follow a less demanding work route until their children were grown, but few make provision for job-sharing or more flexible ways of working at the highest levels.

Women managers need help. They need, like all new and rising managers, a helping hand and a listening ear. They have to overcome prejudice, overt or covert, and their own feelings of isolation. They have few role models to follow and their every step, whether they are tokens or beacons, is watched. They need a space in which they can experiment and a forum to articulate and develop their ideas. Above all, they have to learn to navigate their way around a complex and often alien land, with its own language, culture and customs. Here we have attempted to provide some hints and tips, from our own experience, which we hope will help in that process which is something between assimilation and creativity.

In Chapter One we argue that there is a female style of management and suggest ways in which this style has come about and how women can use it to their own and their organisation's benefit. We are clear that this is not 'power behind the throne'; nor is it to do with manipulation or an air of mystery. We argue that a woman's style and individuality is her strength and that what as women we need to do to get to the top and stay there is to go with, rather than suppress, our individuality.

In Chapter Two we begin to identify some of the areas of work where myths and rituals abound and to guide the woman manager through, as she takes a variety of roles from secretary to chair.

In Chapter Three we look at how men and women

relate at work and show how language and behaviour is interpreted differently by each gender. We argue that the challenge is for us to understand each other and work together for cultural change.

Chapter Four deals with the tricky issue of women working with women, as secretaries or bosses. This area is, in our experience, one fraught with difficulties, as well as benefits and one on which honest discussion is often taboo.

In Chapter Five we examine the complex issues of the boundary between home and work and of the challenges a woman manager faces as she takes on a job which demands a lot of her time and attention.

In Chapter Six we ask whether it is all worth the struggle. Some women are giving up the climb to the top, discouraged by the obstacles and tired of picking out the shards of the 'glass ceiling' which attach themselves as they try to break through. We conclude, overall, that it is worth it and that the personal fulfilment which comes from a responsible job is very satisfying.

Convinced (well, most of the time) as a group of writers that this path is worth pursuing, we take the reader through the preparation for a promotion or career move and look at the interview process which will take her on to the next challenge. The book is therefore intended as a starting point for any woman in management, seeking a management position or for anyone simply interested in the issues facing the woman manager in the 1990s and, we suspect, beyond. The format has been designed so that the book can be read in any order and each chapter stands alone. We have tried to include those practical hints and tips which we have found helpful in our working lives.

We began this book in a spirit of optimism with regards to women in the workplace. The media coverage of the demographic decline which means that more older women will be needed for work and the launch of the Opportunity 2000 programme led many of us to believe that the pressure was on for equality of opportunity at work and that changes in attitudes and cultures were beginning to emerge.

Women have made great progress in their visibility both within society and within the workplace. However, there still exist enormous hurdles and obstacles for women to overcome in order to gain promotion to positions of influence and power. These impediments are all too well-documented. What is not are the ways in which women can break through the invisible yet real 'glass ceiling'. This is our attempt to provide a starting point – from our own varied sets of experience – for women to begin to explore where they are professionally and to identify their own style. We have no magic solutions and we certainly do not have all the answers. What we have, and want to share with the reader, is a firm belief that women can work together to become change-agents. En route there is a lot of hard work and insecurity, but also a lot of fun and fulfilment.

The book has been completed in a climate of deepening economic recession and uncertainty, with companies closing and jobs being lost. Even the optimism around 1992 and an integrated Europe have been overshadowed by political disagreements, civil wars and economic disintegration. It might be argued that in this context the topic of this book is of limited or partial importance. We would argue that the opposite is true. In this time of massive upheaval and reassessment of management practice, it is extremely relevant to look closely at the contribution women, who make up over 50% of the world's population, can make. Any sea change within society can be seen as threatening and as creating insecurities where once all seemed known and safe. The time of retrenchment is over: we can no longer allow ourselves, if we ever could, to stay with old solutions to new problems. We need all the talents that are available to help create a new future. To apply the brakes to women's long march of progress is to limit development and progress at the very time when it is needed.

Each of us writing this book has a demanding job and we met regularly after our separate working days to report on progress and plan the next stage of this book. We met on neutral territory so one of us would not have to cook or make coffee and the one sure way we would find each other in the many and varied venues was to follow the sound of subtle and relieved laughter as we each unloaded our own troubles of the day. This helped us all believe that things can and do change. We were often tired, harassed and under pressure and we learnt that this pressure, when directed towards something we believe in, in this case this book, can be a positive force. Within minutes of meeting we found, through sharing experiences, a new lease of life unimagined on the journey in. From this experience we have found new ways of working with others.

It became very important to hang on to that sound of

laughter as an antidote on those days when we each felt lonely as women in our organisations. We realised that one of the great strengthening experiences was the opportunity to share bits and pieces from our personal and professional lives and to learn that our fears were understood and our hopes shared. For many women managers this is not possible. Hopefully, in sharing our thoughts and fears, this book will become a starting point for other women to enjoy the sound of laughter.

Professor Christine E King, Editor,
Pro-Vice Chancellor,
Staffordshire University 1993

The writing team;
Maureen Atkinson
Joss West-Burnham
Christine King
Angie Robinson

1

A Woman's Way?

'I think all business practices would improve immeasurably if they were guided by 'feminine' principles – qualities like love, and care, and intuition.'

Anita Roddick

Introduction

There is a thesis that suggests that women manage in ways that are distinctive. This 'female' style of management, it is argued, is based on a different set of assumptions about how the world works. There may be many elements of a female style and different women may demonstrate differences in their practices as managers, but nevertheless there is, it is claimed, a set of loosely-shared values that are 'female' and which impact on how a woman relates within an organisation and how she sees and fulfils her role. It is clear that not all women manage in a way that is clearly identifiable as 'female' and that some men do show these traits. Women can also learn men's ways, the argument continues, but may, by learning this behaviour, suppress those very skills and characteristics likely to bring about institutional change, personal success and to add a vital dynamic to teams of men and women working together.

This book aims to examine what, in practice, this 'woman's style' might look like and takes some practical examples of such a style in operation. We attempt to identify some of the traditions and norms of company behaviour, for example in meetings, and ask how women might maximise their contribution. We look at people working together in teams, at women as leaders and women as colleagues.

We ask questions about possible differences between men and women in the ways that they view inter-personal relationships. This chapter begins by identifying some commonly-held assumptions about what it means to be a manager and how women figure in this scenario.

The Cultural Context of Management

It is not by accident that most books and articles on management refer to the manager as male. One such book, widely-available at railway station bookstalls, offers two versions; one is a guidebook for the business-man and one is for the businesswoman. Only the covers are different; the text is the same, as are the references to the manager throughout as 'he'. The image we have within our society of the manager is male and this, in itself, can be a barrier to women seeing themselves in management roles. When it comes to senior manage-ment positions, there are even fewer positive images for women and 'being the boss' may represent an alien and worrying role for a woman, who would see herself as isolated and in a situation which is stressful because it is different from the assumed norm of what women have been or can be. From the beginnings of her thinking about a career these kinds of stereotypes may act as subtle barriers to her aspirations. A woman's own self-image may, therefore, be in conflict with her ambition and may prevent her from setting herself clear goals.

The effect of these influences should not be underestimated, although we are generalising and recognise that there are exceptions and subtle shifts of expectations within society. On the whole, and crudely, however, women, from the day that they are born, have to find their way through a culture that assigns them a particular set of roles and values and which identifies them as different from men and, in many ways, 'lesser'. We suggest that within the workplace, as women managers, we need to hold firm to our different perspective, being clear that this does not make us less valuable or able, just different. This vision is needed to counteract the views held, amongst both women and men, that women are not ambitious and would rather follow than lead.

In part, some of these stereotypes have come about precisely because of the expectations that men and women are essentially different. Old arguments that men are naturally tough, strong and independent and that women are weak, caring and dependent still have a strong hold on the world of employment. The kinds of jobs women have traditionally taken and their predominance within the 'support' and 'service' areas reinforces these often unarticulated assumptions. They certainly have an effect on how women think about themselves and prompt the feeling that 'I'm not strong enough/good enough/ ambitious enough to do that job . . .' Women, like men, can be and are independent, strong and caring and if they sometimes express these characteristics in different ways from men, then the trick is to recognise and value both the skills and the way in which they are expressed. The qualities are important irrespective of gender. The forms of expression may vary and this variation is valuable. What may be seen as 'weakness' in a woman may be the demonstration of a particular and necessary skill, but shown in a way that does not fit the expectations of the norms, which we have argued are predominantly male, of the world of work. In the perceived 'weaknesses' of women may lie those very skills which leading figures in the world of organisations are arguing that we need for the 1990s and beyond. The traditional undervaluing of women's skills needs to be recognised, as organisations seek to manage rapid change and need radical and effective managers of resources and people. As women need to learn and develop some of the skills shown by men at work, so men, we suggest, would become more successful managers if they felt able to display their 'female' traits of care and nurture.

Management as Male? The Story so Far . . .

We would argue that within most organisations the dominant culture is male. This is not simply reflected in the predominance of men in senior positions, but in the very assumptions about ways of working, from the timing of meetings to the criteria for making new appointments. The structures work on assumptions that are usually unconscious but which expect that most employees, and certainly most senior employees, will be men. Daily timetables, working practices and styles and career paths are mapped out to fit male needs and expectations. It is perhaps not surprising that the idea persists that women are not ambitious. It has been pointed out in a variety of studies on women and work that this myth is a comfortable one for those who already have power, since it allows employers to exclude women without feeling any guilt. It is then that we hear the familiar and plaintive cries: 'They don't apply . . .', 'They are their own worst enemies . . .' and so on.

In Came the Women

The entry of women into management positions over the last thirty years in greater numbers has lead to a questioning of these assumptions. Women managers have had, and still have, a major part to play in implementing change. Whilst there are male managers in the vanguard of change, it is perhaps not surprising, since most managers are men, that the amount of sympathy and priority given to equal opportunities programmes is likely to be limited.

Some men are, of course, committed to equal opportunities and recognise the implications for working practices and company culture. Others are less convinced but can see the pragmatic benefits as we move into a time when women workers and especially women returners will be an important part of the workforce. Many organisations have policy statements and practices on equal opportunities but these vary in their effectiveness. Few are willing to radically review the situation for women or undertake positive action programmes to help women 'catch up' with their male colleagues. The very phrase 'positive discrimination', even if it is not fully understood, is enough to send some people, both men and women, into a panic.There are differences between countries; clearly the United States is more advanced in much of its practice in this area. Europe has further to go. Neither can be complacent. There are companies where 'positive action' programmes are avoided and as a consequence women can neither take appropriate training nor become visible as contenders for top jobs. The world of management is thereby depriving itself of a pool of talent of people who can make an important difference to an organisation's future.

The 1990 Hansard Society Commission Report[1] on women in top management jobs aimed to discover why there remains a consistent under-representation of women in senior positions within the British Isles. The report was able to point to a variety of reasons and these include out-dated attitudes towards women's roles in society, inadequate provision for the care of children or other dependants and a lack of flexibility in organisations. One year on, the report's findings were investigated in a newspaper survey on women and work which suggested that a majority of women do not believe that there have been significant changes either in men's attitudes or in discrimination in the workplace in the last 21 years.

These surveys are reinforced in the autobiographical writings of successful women who have worked against the grain. Anita Roddick, for example, maintains that women do not stand a chance in business as it is organised at the moment:

'The reason is that corporations are largely created by men for men, often influenced by military or public school models. Hierarchical structures built on authority remain unchanged and many men find it difficult to accept the rise of women to top management positions-perhaps because they have never learned to deal with women other than as secretaries, wives, girlfriends, mothers, daughters or adjuncts to themselves.'[2]

Anita Roddick is clear that women face enormous hurdles in these structures, where the criteria for promotion are based on male values. She points out that much business is undertaken in male gatherings, either formal or informal, and women are excluded from such discussions.

The Woman as Manager

A woman who finds herself, not withstanding this glass ceiling, in a position of power within a male culture often feels that her presence is in itself perceived as 'unusual'. At the very least, she is highly visible, in her presence or absence, her voice at meetings is clearly different and she may either be ignored or given the kind of intense and curious attention that denies her the safety from discovery of the mistakes that we all make but which for men are normally less obvious.

It is hardly surprising to find that many women, on being promoted, are sent speedily on a course to learn how to be a manager. These are normally courses designed by and for men and the message is that women need to learn company codes and rules. Whilst all managers may need to learn to negotiate their way through an organisational culture, both men and women have more to give to their companies and colleagues if they can express their own views and bring their own perspectives to bear. We want to encourage women and men to accept the validity of differences and women, in particular, to believe in themselves and their ways of working. Such personal empowerment is the first step towards the empowerment of others and the management of the many changes which organisations need in order to survive and flourish in the current economic and social climate.

A Woman's Style

In this chapter we have argued that female and male management styles are intrinsically different and that these differences stem from the culture into which we are born and brought up. We are encouraging women to believe in and develop their own style, rather than to learn to suppress these differences. As we look more closely at ways in which women behave in companies, we recognise the differences between women and acknowledge that women have a variety of ways of working. These differences come not only from personal background but also from the need for women to adapt their ways variously to fit the world in which they live and work.

The Woman as Chameleon

Every age believes that it is seeing more rapid and challenging changes than before. Yet for managers it would seem that the 1990s require special and specific skills and talents to facilitate in creative ways the very rapid changes society and the world of work is witnessing. Many women are, we would argue, particularly well-equipped to cope with and manage change in a variety of social, domestic and work contexts. Women learn, from a young age, to adapt to society's expectations of them; they are often flexible and unconstrained by traditional practices and their very ignorance of the rites and rituals of male groups will allow them to think around problems and find what are sometimes radical solutions.

Thus we see flexibility as a key strength for the woman manager; as a chameleon she can tailor her behaviour and language to the situation she finds herself in. Her adaptability, provided it allows her freedom to implement her own solutions and does not involve denial of her individuality, can bring her great success. There are dangers, however, and it might be useful at this stage to look at some of the positive benefits of this style of working, and some of the risks.

The chameleon woman manager has STRENGTHS in that she is:

- flexible
- democratic
- sensitive to culture changes.

Others may see these characteristics as WEAK-NESSES:

- flexibility may be seen as a lack of direction
- democracy may appear to be time-wasting and not appropriate behaviour for a leader
- she may be seen as inconsistent and therefore not trustworthy

There are, however, many OPPORTUNITIES:

- the chameleon manager keeps others on their toes— nothing is taken for granted!
- she may persuade others to be more open to new ideas and others' views
- she makes people feel valued and listened to
- she can help create a culture change in organisations.

The THREATS come from others' perceptions and, often, the lack of women colleagues or peers who are willing to advise on how she is being perceived.

- her openness can be abused by others, men and women
- she can lose sight of what specific actions need to be taken
- she can be seen as 'too casual'.

Many of her problems are ones of perception rather than reality. She may doubt herself and her own ways of working; others may see as weaknesses in her what appear as strengths in a man. Marilyn Loden[3] tells us how some people think they can tell a businessman from a businesswoman. A businessman, for example, is aggressive whilst a businesswoman is pushy. He is good on details whilst she is nit-picking. He knows when to persist, she doesn't know when to stop. He is a man of the world but she has 'been around'. Colleagues see him as a stern taskmaster but she is difficult to work for.

However hard it is for the successful woman to overcome her own fears, and deal with the prejudices of others, we would argue that this ingredient of flexibility is a real bonus for the aspirant woman manager in the 1990s. Many commentators agree that the macho management styles of the 80s have largely failed. Where they have brought change it is often superficial and people have failed to take ownership. A style of working which is hierarchical and inflexible is now widely seen to be inappropriate to the 90s and companies and institutions are increasingly looking for, and perhaps for the first time giving credit to, managers who are flexible and able to adapt.

Jane McLoughlin[4], in her interviews with successful women managers, suggests that we have to take on board the fact that women themselves have also undergone tremendous change with regard to their roles in society. At one level there are changes that liberate women and bring recognition that they may have ambitions and careers. The image of the working woman now appears in advertising and the media and the challenging of old stereotypes is to be celebrated. Some women are warning, however, that these changes bring paradoxes. The stereotypical woman of the coffee advertisement is not only successful, beautiful and sexy but she also showers her attention on her man. The 'superwoman syndrome' can present impossible pressures for women and turn into another 'glass ceiling', a barrier barely visible to outsiders but real enough to those of us who try to do everything perfectly. *Cosmopolitan* may have told us in the 1980s that we could 'have everything' but we have subsequently learnt that, when a woman pursues a career, serious changes and serious choices have to be made in her life.

If, for now, we accept the premise that society is changing in its views about women's roles, then we can see that women themselves are driving these changes in practical ways. Women are, we have argued, particularly good change-agents but need, in order to be wholly effective, to have support. One of the major problems for the woman who wants to implement changes is her isolation. This will remain until there is a critical mass of women in a variety of key areas who are working to create change. We are nowhere near that situation yet but what we are seeing is a wider acknowledgement that male managers also have a feminine side that can be tapped to great effect in their business activities. McLouglin suggests that:

> 'A lot of management training and theory now are in fact the feminine way of doing things. Traditional practice was strong, authoritarian, combative and now what a lot of training does is advocate communication and leading by example.'[5]

Throughout the book we aim to exemplify other characteristics of a woman's style. Besides flexibility, many people would identify the importance of women's interpersonal and communications skills. Women are seen, at best, to lead by example and to be especially good at building efficient and effective teams. Women, working within their own range of styles, will seek to ensure, in the main, co-operation rather than competition within the workplace. Co-operation can be shown to work, although it appears to challenge a premise of the traditional business world that senior managers are characterised by their ability to 'win at all costs'. Clearly there is a place for competition but a challenge to the concept that competition and 'victory' should drive organisational life can be very liberating and bring all sorts of benefits. Internal co-operation to strengthen a company for external competition offers a dynamic way forward. This is visible within Japanese firms where the influence of the culture of Zen Buddhism has infiltrated management thinking and practices. It is interesting for our purposes to note that some of the principles of Zen reflect those characteristics we are identifying as important (although not exclusive) to women. These might include:

- patience
- observation
- stability
- nurturing
- communication.

As Japanese firms, with demonstrable success, value what we in the West see as 'soft', then those 'female' characteristics, whether shown by men or women, may move to the centre of our stage. 'Softness' may be seen to represent a different kind of strength; one that is calm, thoughtful and secure. As Jane McLoughlin tells us[6] 'Confidence is the *key* factor for every woman in management. If you have the confidence to want to realise your own vision of management, you seek the authority to do so.' Women, as managers, want to the get the job done. Our motto might be: 'Let's do it and let's do it differently!'

Notes

1. *Women at the Top,* Hansard Society, London, 1990.
2. Roddick, A., *Body and Soul,* Edbury Press, London, 1991, p.216.
3. Loden, M., *Feminine Leadership or How to Succeed in Business Without Being One of the Boys,* Times Books, New York, 1985, p.38.
4. McLoughlin, J., *Up and Running, Women in Business,* Virago, London, 1992, *passim.*
5. *Ibid.,* p. 26.
6. McLoughlin, J., *op. cit.,* p. 56.

2

Women and Meetings

'Fifty people at the meeting –
I want to say something,
but is it relevant,
and is it pertinent . . .?
. . . Was it OK?
Tell me – how did I sound?
                                    Natasha Josefowitz

Introduction

Much of a manager's time, indeed some would say too much, is spent in meetings. These can be highly productive vehicles for communication and decision making. Equally, they can be occasions that are stressful, frustrating and just plain boring. In this chapter we look at the ways in which women can capitalise on their personal skills to get the best out of meetings and to make the most effective contribution, whether in the chair, acting as secretary or simply as a member.

Meetings: Acting as Chair

The secret of successful chairing is preparation. It is important to ensure that the preparatory tasks are shared with others and that the discussions and decisions are jointly owned. In this way women operate what men might see as a 'lobby', but, instead of concentrating on one desired result, they will aim to see that the experience itself is a positive one and that the outcome is one that can be agreed and collectively delivered. The best meetings have members who are unambiguous about their tasks, have a precise set of aims and who feel comfortable in making a contribution. Good meetings end with members clear about what has been decided and what action is to be taken by whom and when. The best meetings inspire those who have taken part to further thought or action around the issues that have been addressed.

Helping to bring about this end requires some simple measures on behalf of the chair. She must know who is attending and ensure that they, especially if they are new to the meeting or in some other way likely to feel ill-at-ease, know what is expected of them. In sharing the responsibility for new or junior members with more established participants, in a mentoring guise, she is helping a wide range of people take responsibility for the meeting's success. Care needs to be taken on the physical arrangements; how the room is laid out and where people are seated is critical. Meetings arranged at a round table, if this is practicable, have a more co-operative air. Meetings in large rooms may mean that some are excluded or intimidated, simply by where they sit. Participants who cannot easily catch the chair's eye, or whose disaffection or disagreement, expressed in their body language, is not read by the chair may end up as, at worst, disruptive and at best, disenchanted.

Everyone needs to feel they are included and are important. If you have to move the furniture to achieve this, then do it!

The social context of meetings is important and is an area where women may put in much effort, often only to be criticised for being too frivolous. Nevertheless, it is worth being at the meeting early to chat to people and to set an atmosphere that is relaxed and friendly. Tea-breaks where people leave their seats to collect their tea can ease tension for everyone and allow the chair to shift the direction of the meeting. Members can relax over the break and difficult people or situations can be negotiated in less confrontational circumstances. This can be seen as time-wasting and women talking in a friendly way to participants may be seen to be 'gossiping'. Seeking a warm and collaborative atmosphere by caring for the comfort and feelings of members is, however, an effective way of achieving results.

Many meetings are too long and are vehicles for senior colleagues to establish their position in the hierarchy by long speeches or the production of long papers. We would recommend that the chair declares the length of the meeting at the beginning or, even better, in the papers which are circulated beforehand. Normally, what cannot be done in two hours needs more than one meeting. If the agenda, papers and minutes are brief and action-centred, the tone of the meeting will follow. It is important to recognise that, traditionally, information was seen as power and often withheld unnecessarily, or dressed up in a way that made it difficult for more junior people to decode. Obviously, some information is confidential, but much is not and women, perhaps because they have been so long 'outsiders' at the most senior levels, do not tend to see their power in these ways. Where they do and where they learn to ape the traditional male ways, they are often less effective than the men and certainly far less practised!

A Key Strength

Women as chairs plan ahead, anticipating success, and capitalise on their relevant strengths, which include working with people and negotiating and sharing goals and achievements.

Meetings: Handling Contributions

Here the woman chair's STRENGTHS become clear. The woman chair is well attuned to signals and she makes space for members to speak. She notices and tries to take action when someone fails to contribute or is withdrawn. Above all, her behaviour indicates that it is safe to talk and her body language and tone of voice will be encouraging. Women will check regularly, as they do in conversation, for a shared understanding of what is happening and will aim towards regular summaries of progress, again checking for agreement and understanding. Like any good chair she will listen but, unlike many men who chair meetings, she is often more flexible and will let a meeting 'flow' whilst keeping a clear control over the process.

A Word of Encouragement

The meetings chaired by a woman often rapidly develop an air of informality. However, the meetings will remain action-oriented. Their strength lies in everyone knowing that they can have their say and that they will be heard. People have even been heard to come out of a meeting chaired in this careful way, whether by a woman or a man, and say that they actually enjoyed it! Having enjoyed the experience, they are that much more committed to the outcomes.

There are WEAKNESSES inherent in such a style, however, and we turn to these next. There is a real tension between giving people their space and voice and effective time management. An arena that is safe can be abused by the long-winded or those with a lot of trees to describe and no sense of the wood. Sometimes a woman chair is deliberately challenged in this way and she has to balance her openness with firmness and an unwillingness to have the meeting used for other purposes. These are the kind of issues and people to be dealt with outside the meeting, but sometimes they can wreck a good session and the blame will fall not on them but on the chair for being too 'weak'. If a meeting does go wrong the male chair will normally assert himself firmly, and thereby silence not only the troublemakers but others. He will rarely see the failed meeting as his fault and will talk, from the chair, to try to establish his authority. Women chairs report that they speedily blame themselves if a meeting starts to feel uncomfortable and thereby lose that very confidence that is the essence of their style of chairing.

A Warning

The need that we all have to be liked can weigh heavily in a meeting and it is sometimes easy to get things completely out of proportion. Remember, you can't win all the time! When a woman chair has lost direction of the meeting it is often more difficult for her to get back on track. Try not to panic; everyone has at least one meeting where this has happened to them. It is not the end of the world and will give useful lessons on how not to get into this position again.

When meetings are not or appear not to be controlled, some members can get nervous. Even a successful meeting chaired by a woman can be seen by some as a talk-shop. It is important to stress the decisions and actions which result from the meeting, even if these are as intangible as having given people a chance to formulate or hear new views. Be brief, be alert and never relax your attention in a meeting you are chairing. With confidence and experience and the carefully nurtured support of some of your members you will be able to overcome the prejudices of others.

Meetings provide a range of OPPORTUNITIES for a woman to demonstrate that her style is effective. Good, relaxed meetings can help to change organisational culture. It is interesting to watch people coming out of meetings tired and confused. By tone of voice and body language it is easy to check on what has gone on. People coming from meetings chaired in a positive way are more likely to be still talking about issues related to the meeting and behaving in more relaxed and social ways than those who have sat through long and formal diatribes. Many women's meetings do produce this good effect and it is important for the chair to watch and listen as another way of obtaining feedback.

There are THREATS and a few pitfalls that the woman manager has to be aware of. Informal control of meetings is a skill and it is hard to learn with few role models around. In your early days of chairing, try this approach, but cautiously. Undertake training if you feel this would help, but take care that you are not simply taught the 'old' ways. You must develop your own style.

And finally, Colleagues . . .

In this, as in other areas of management, you will sometimes get it wrong. There is nothing worse than having chaired a meeting and having failed to resolve the issues at stake. The potential for self-blame is enormous and your attendees will all be there to help pile the coals onto your fire of guilt. However, all is not lost and if you learn from your mistakes and get some first aid (friends outside work are a help here – or perhaps a swim, a novel or a long walk!). Seek support from your team if you have one; if not, build one. Next we look at two more roles which women take in meetings: acting as secretary and where they are team members rather than team leaders.

Acting as a Meeting Secretary

It is not necessary to convince most meetings that the role of secretary should be taken by a woman. This is what people are used to; what women do, what they should do, what they do best, what they have always been allowed to do. Whilst we might take issue with some of the assumptions here, clearly most women are extremely good at being meeting secretaries. They bring a range of STRENGTHS to the task and the success of the meeting and its outcomes can be largely in their hands. These strengths might include an ability

- to look a problem from several angles
- to anticipate issues and problems likely to arise
- to provide efficient and supportive help to the chair
- to prepare for the meeting, both in terms of the paper-work and for members' comfort ('meetings always start well because Jane has thought to reserve car parking spaces!').

Throughout the meeting the secretary's ability to do several things at once is an asset. The skilled secretary will be listening and recording the discussions as well as keeping an eye on delegates, prompting the chair and distributing papers. In some meetings, she will also be contributing to discussions.

A Few Comments

'The best minute-takers we have met are women.'

'We're criticised as women for verbosity but when it comes to the minutes of meetings, clear summaries and action points,we get it done!'

'We make excellent minute-takers because we listen well, our records are detailed and we can summarise and present these clearly.'

'We act as interpreters and translators of meeting-speak.'

'We're good because we've had over a hundred years of practice!'

There are some real dangers and WEAKNESSES inherent in these time-honoured skills. A secretary, notwithstanding the centrality of her role, can be and often is invisible. In a meeting dominated by men she is cast in the role of 'server' and the stereotype of the one woman manager at a senior meeting; taking the minutes and also pouring the tea is, sadly, not yet a redundant joke. Even amongst peers, the sole woman often finds herself acting in a secretarial role. We may even find ourselves volunteering, either to quell fears that we are 'too feminist' or to find a role in which we are comfortable. In such a situation 'serving' the meeting may impose a rule of silence on the secretary. Organisations have histories and cultural expectations about roles and hierarchies. A meeting, especially at senior level, can highlight the status of participants and the behaviour in that meeting may take the form of a ritual dance. Speaking up is hard if people expect you to be silent. So many secretaries leave meetings 'dying to say something' but feel that they dare not. For the woman working with male peers, the advantages of the secretarial role may well not be worth the penalty of being seen but not heard. For those who are less senior than others at the meeting, a word with a sympathetic chair beforehand might just create the opportunity to pass an opinion. Women in the chair have a special responsibility to include their meeting secretaries in the discussion and often find a valuable and perceptive contributor.

Alongside the dangers come new OPPOR-TUNITIES. The meeting secretary is often a role women feel comfortable with. We may hate taking minutes as a technical activity, but the secretary's role is one that we can and are allowed to slot into comfortably. It is one of the classic female stereotypes, but it does allow access to information and powerful people. Wisely used, as a springboard rather than a shelter, it can prove a useful tool in career development. Knowledge of the formal and informal rules of meetings can be very empowering and, since women bosses will almost certainly be working with female secretaries, it is a great strength if they can understand and practice the task they are asking others to do with and for them.

The THREAT is a simple one; that you are backed into a corner and made to take on the role whether or not you are the most appropriate person. Once there, the group can marginalise you. 'Give her hands something to do and it will keep her mouth shut!' is a principle that we have all probably seen applied more than once.

A Word of Advice

You must consider carefully whether you want to play

this role, how you play it and how you will be allowed to play it. There is a good chance you will volunteer because women managers are good at that.

Being a Contributor

Meetings provide a platform; contributing in a meeting is a very powerful way of communicating and of being noticed, but if you do not learn the rules of the game you can fail or not even be allowed to play. Rule one, as we have indicated above, is about the relative status of participants and the recognition that, for some of them, position overrides anything a more junior person might say. You have to judge where you are and how far you go with or flout the conventions. Women's voices in meetings are still, in many cases, so rare that they are heard, if not always listened to, so you have an advantage. The disadvantage is that this visibility robs you of the inalienable right of every participant to get something wrong. Your mistakes and hesitations will be remembered. Luckily, women are astute enough to judge the situation and flexible enough to change tack, if necessary, as they go along.

Men, whether as children in school or managers in meetings, always surround a question with a statement. They take space and draw attention to themselves, marking their place in, or claim to a place in, the hierarchy. We tend to ask the short, straightforward question and, if we are the only one doing it this way, our straightforwardness will be taken for ignorance. It is a kind of ignorance of the golden rule of meetings, 'never say simply what you can dress up', but it is perhaps a rule best ignored. We need to make our points simply and confidently and keep at it until the meeting gets used to our style. If there are other women or sympathetic men present, get them to do what men do all the time in meetings, reinforce your point by repeating it, preferably using your name at the same time: 'As Mary has just suggested. . . .'

Some tips to help you make the most of the meetings you attend:

- be sure why you are there. Are you there representing yourself or others?
- are you prepared? Have you read the papers and do you know where you might make a comment?
- can you deal with public criticism or disagreement? If not, get some help or training.
- can you argue a point without being out of control? If not, deal with this!
- can you cope when someone steals your idea? There are strategies you can learn and practice.
- can you resist jumping to your feet to hand round the coffee?
- do you know and follow the codes of behaviour: on dress, for example (a suit means business, a suit jacket kept on gives you authority) and on the language of the meeting (is it formal or informal; do you sit or stand to make your point?)
- can you project your voice without waivering? If not, get some help.

Meetings can be your platform. At the very least you can learn and observe. Seek feedback and find areas where you can make a contribution. Women are so visible that there will be interest or at least curiosity in what you say. Practice, through your meetings, getting the content style and tone right and you are on your way to having your own meetings to chair.

3

Women and Men Working together

'We live in reference to past experience and not to future events.'

H. G. Wells

Introduction

There are very few working environments that are single-sexed. The way in which women and men relate in the work place is critical to many of the issues with which we are concerned here. We will look in this chapter at a number of issues, ranging from those of language and communication to those of expectations and perceptions. We ask what it means to 'play the boys' game' and what it means to be a woman boss. All of these questions are set for women and men in a context of rapid social change, with all the associated opportunities and threats.

In one sense the workplace is now more welcoming for women. Demographic patterns mean that their contribution is essential and equal opportunities legislation has brought some cultural and organisational shifts. Other changes are being brought about by market forces, international and particularly Japanese ways of working. Some organisations are undergoing a review of their structures and taking on board the move towards a company culture that is more caring towards the environment and towards its people. Macho management style is identified, at least in the class-rooms of the Business Schools, as being out of fashion, whilst care for people, team working and an open management style is identified as best for business. For many writers within the field of management develop-ment, the 'greedy' culture of the 80s and the hard-nosed management practices associated with this are viewed as fundamentally unsound. There are many voices arguing for a new approach to managing and leader-ship. Marilyn Loden[1] suggests that 'Feminine and masculine styles are necessary for a holistic approach, taking full advantage of the entire spectrum of human talents.' Never has the need to review our working practices been stronger, yet women's contributions are still not being fully used.

Those who are heard to say, when asked why their senior management teams have no or few women members, 'but women simply don't apply!' are also apt to tell us that 'this is work, gender is irrelevant.' We all bring to work, however, the people that we are, and our gender differences, perhaps even more than our social differences, underpin our attitudes and behaviour. Indeed, the complimentary attitudes and approaches of men and women professionals can bring to an organisa-tion that very dynamic that allows it to work in new ways and achieve its greatest potential. There are, of course, problems and conflicts and a great number of crossed communication lines, but there are very positive ways forward which do not mean that women have to change their style and learn new rules.

The discussion is still relatively new. In their work on management in education, Riches and Morgan suggest that 'even in mainstream management thinking, the gender issues in management . . . have only just begun to surface'.[2]

This avoidance or ignorance of the relevance of gender issues is apparent as we look at various management models that see no relevance in the argument that language, culture, training and structures are important to a company that wishes to be healthily balanced in gender and in its attitudes. Thus the 'woman manager' in such a model has to learn to be a 'proper' manager and the company need make no changes to reflect her presence.

Gender, we are arguing, is an issue and most women managers would, we feel, agree. Even admitting this can be, for both men and women, a threatening experience. Men are faced with asking fundamental questions and with making changes and women have to deal with the fact that their difference will not, whatever they do, be forgotten by their male colleagues. This is, perhaps, particularly hard for women who will insist 'I want to be judged on my merit; this has nothing to do with me being a woman.' Nevertheless, our codes of behaviour, from dress to body language, are different and how we look, what we say and what we do are judged by standards that are laden with social and gender meanings and values.

We go on to examine some of the elements that relate centrally to issues of gender in the workplace.

Chair or Chairman – Does Language Matter?

The most important part of management, it could be argued, is communication – both in listening and informing. A sign of an efficient and successful organisation is one where messages, information, knowledge and ideas are communicated in such a way that a shared understanding can be built. At the core of communications are the verbal and non-verbal codes we use to convey our meaning.

Some words convey more than one layer of meaning and some of these connotations may work against us. Not only do we have the expectation that certain jobs belong to men in words like **man**agement or chair**man,** but also the assumptions associated with a range of more seemingly gender-free words. Archer and Lloyd, in *Sex and Gender*[3], list some examples.

MEN	WOMEN
aggressive	affectionate
ambitious	emotional
assertive	gentle
competitive	caring
dominant	submissive
forceful	obedient
self-confidant	anxious
independent	dependent
decisive	indecisive

You may not agree or you may wish to make additions or substitutions. We all use shorthand to make sense of our environment. Stereotypes serve a purpose, in that they simplify complex sets of information. Where individuals or groups do not fit the shorthand they are seen as deviating from the norm. What was a useful tool can quickly become a basis for judgement or discrimination and language as a tool of communication has failed.

We are suggesting, throughout this book, that women as managers have found new ways of working which challenge, either deliberately or unconsciously, the accepted norms. Language and issues of understanding and being understood affect our behaviour and success in meetings, interviews, telephone conversations, face to face confrontations and team work, as well as many other situations.

Understanding Each Other

Language used in the workplace can help form or reinforce views about the right way to do things. At a simple level we often find that the language of organisations praises people for behaving 'like a man' or being 'one of the guys'. Does it feel the same when we praise a man by describing his execution of a task as having been done 'just like a woman' or congratulate a man for being 'one of the girls'?

Men and women can mean different things by the same language. This area has been covered by Deborah Tanner who gives some fascinating examples in her book, *You Just Don't Understand: Women and Men in Conversation.*

Marilyn Loden in *Feminine Leadership or How to Succeed in Business Without Being One of the Boys*, also investigates this area, stressing that the cultures of the workplace have been largely formed by male values and language. Loden maintains that 'the corporate culture that women managers encounter has been entirely shaped by men' and goes on to use the term originally coined by Betty Friedan in her article 'Twenty Years after the Feminine Mystique' in the New York Times, 1983, of the 'male-centred culture and ambience'. Loden suggests that at the heart of the corporate world is 'competitiveness' – that 'all business, all of life, is an ongoing competition' and that the goal is always to 'win'. As a consequence, much of the language is military with the use of metaphors of battles, strategy, game plans and targets. All these lay the foundations for 'the rules of the game'. Since many boy's games are concerned with warfare, not welfare, the links are clear. Somewhere along the way management language has been intertwined with the language of sport and war which does have that element of 'gamesmanship' and which women often find less than comfortable.

Learning the language is about as much help to a woman as wearing her pin-striped suit; it may provide a little camouflage, but will not disguise the fact that she is different. We are on difficult ground because it is apparent that, regardless of how adaptable some may be, women are still women. Even when they attempt to behave exactly like their male counterparts, others still view them differently.

Think for a moment how the woman manager who uses strong language or, to use the military analogy, 'swears like a trooper', is perceived. Usually she is seen as 'hard' and 'a bitch'. If she offers 'feminine style' above a certain level in the organisation, she will be seen as a 'bimbo' and not fit for management. A way men use to put women down at work, either deliberately or without thinking, is to address them in terms like 'love' and 'dear' that is the language of familiarity and reinforces the assumption of the woman's lower place in the hierarchy. Whilst the woman manager who does not object may be seen as 'reasonable' and 'not one of those feminists', it will also be assumed that she knows her place and will almost certainly stay there.

Action

It is in the interest of organisations to work on their corporate language and women managers within the system may want to initiate or assist in this process. Rather than offer what might be seen as a critical concern with the trivial, women need to seek senior allies, male or female, and explain the advantages of a company taking care of its language. We have already argued that the best organisations are those which communicate well, both up and down. Few companies, we have agreed, employ only men or only women, looking across the range of jobs, so clearly there is an argument for change. A shared language facilitates a shared identity and a shared culture and promotes a sense of belonging. The discussions around the changes in style and language can, in themselves, remove barriers and enable people to work together in new ways. Any worker has the right not to be subject to insult or harassment, and ensuring this at a level deeper than the more obvious is good management practice.

There are risks. Language, as we have seen, can enshrine our deepest prejudices and challenging these feels risky. Reviewing language and style can be seen as a fad or as a waste of valuable company time. Most managers, however, can spot an idea that helps their organisation develop; that is why they are managers. By appealing to the practical rather than the moral argument, change can be achieved, sometimes with the most surprising champions.

Just as language can limit and define us, so do people's expectations of each other. Most women in the average male manager's life are in a special kind of relationship to him, as, for example, wife, mother or secretary. We look next at what happens when he has to see her in a new role, as his professional peer or superior. How does the man who has a woman boss view her?

Men with Women Bosses

Many men do, of course, work well with their woman boss and find her style of working empowers them. They may have no hang-ups that interfere with their professional relationships and are fortunate in having a woman boss who is good at her job. Many, however, have serious problems, and the majority it would seem, talking to a range of men and women, have some degree of problem. Here are some of the phrases that we have heard or have had reported to us as male judgements on female achievement.

- petticoat tyranny
- she slept her way up
- she stole what was mine
- who does she think she is?
- hard as nails
- she isn't married you know (i.e. isn't a real woman)
- she won't be able to handle those men
- there will be tears!
- reminds me of my mother
- not much older than my daughter
- now she'll appoint more of her own
- she wouldn't know a management strategy even if she had the recipe
- when the going gets tough she'll be off
- she's pre-menstrual/ menopausal/menstrual . . .
- she'll learn.

Let us hope they give her the chance to learn! The list is long and we could all add to it, perhaps from our own experience. Some of these statements are unthinking but draw, nevertheless, on primitive stereotypes that define woman as a sexual object. Many such statements draw on models of women and their roles in society, as mother, lover, temptress, and so on. As women we often collude to greater or lesser degrees in these female stereotypes. We stereotype men and their reactions, often misunderstanding them and misreading the signals or reacting at work to a comment that touches a raw point from our private lives. Criticism at work may strike at the very root of our self-confidence, because it appears to touch the woman we are and this shaking of the foundations can spill over into or from our personal lives. As women we are often hard on other women, having been taught to see them as social and sexual competitors. Some of the comments about women bosses above came from women.

There has been a recent court case in England on what was asserted to be the unequal treatment of a woman for a professional 'misdemeanour'. The woman in question, who was in a senior position in the public sector, had stripped to her underwear to swim with male colleagues and had a drink whilst on duty .What happened to her male colleagues, one might wonder, who were similarly 'unprofessional'? The case caused widespread interest and the key issue, of the woman's lost promotion, was forgotten in the coverage as her image, language and behaviour as a woman was paraded for everyone to view with as much detailed voyeurism as was currently being accorded to the British royal princesses. The case died quietly and the end was a disappointment to many women and men who had hoped to see some recognition of the issues. Her acceptance of early retirement on health grounds left her career finished. Others will need to take up the struggle for equal treatment.

Whilst we cannot control how others see us or prevent them from labelling and misjudging us, we can be aware of ways in which we can manage those reactions without losing our faith in ourselves. By example, by steady success, a woman manager can win allies and she can change the culture that allows superficial judgements and where those who mock are the heroes. Fundamental to this is how you feel about yourself. Lois Wyse in her book *The Six Figure Woman* (*and how to be one*) says,

> 'I would advise a woman starting out. . . to become comfortable with being a woman, to be comfortable with her body and her mind. Also to be aware of the special sensitivity that women have, their ability to make things happen'

and we would whole-heartedly endorse this. There is an ancient Arab saying: 'Trust in God and tie up your camel'; we would say: on the one hand trust your own instincts in the workplace – on the other be on your guard.

In summary, there are STRENGTHS in being aware of how others may see you. These include:

- your listening and attention to the care of others is a sign of good management
- it can increase your self-knowledge and self confidence
- you can learn new things about yourself
- working together is better than working alone.

There are WEAKNESSES also:

- criticisms can be taken too personally and can be undermining
- facing up to anger and envy can produce an emotional reaction in you
- you may be tempted to be reactive rather than proactive.

The **OPPORTUNITIES** are important:

- rather than relying on power which comes from your position, you can gain power based on your personal understanding and relationships
- through identifying how you are seen, you will identify areas of the organisation's culture where changes would bring about healthier and more productive ways of working
- by facing up to others' comments, you can build long-term trust and build on genuinely shared values.

And there are **THREATS**:

- some people perceive that 'personal' issues are not the concern of the workplace
- you can feel frustration at the way you are misunderstood
- change takes time and the process of waiting for the 'breakthrough' can be painful.

We did warn you to be on your guard!

Playing the Boys' Game

We have argued so far in this chapter that language and men's views of women managers together help to create the environment in which women work and are judged on their style and performance alongside their male colleagues. It could be argued that women are judged on whether they can play the game the way men can.

There is a body of evidence that questions the fairness to women both of appraisal schemes and of psycho-metric and diagnostic tests. Who is to judge how a woman manager is succeeding?

There are situations where women managers are perceived as alien and their 'success' is judged on the speed with which they learn the rules and how to 'fit in'. One managing director commented on the appoint-ment of a senior woman manager that 'only the plumbing will change around here.'

The assumption is that women are outsiders and have to learn to become insiders. There is rarely, and perhaps understandably, given the rarity of senior women in corporations, a question raised about whether the organisation should change or adapt.

These issues are discussed by Marilyn Loden in *Feminine Leadership* and by Betty Harragan in *Games Mother Never Taught You*. Both suggest that women are provided with very little space to negotiate being themselves or bringing their own styles into play. They map out a scenario that goes something like this: little girls are socialised into being caring, unselfish, quiet and obedient. They move, through their careers, into a situation where they learn to operate more like men, but do this so gradually that they begin to modify their individuality. All the literature of success tells them they must be more strategic, aggressive, competitive and less emotional and sensitive. Holding on to that which makes you strong and effective as an individual, at work or at home, is difficult under the barrage of advice that tells us to change.

Some women have paid a high price for their senior

positions and their success needs to be acknowledged and respected. For change to happen, however, women have to enter senior management positions in large numbers. To achieve this there have to be changes in thinking and perception with respect to management as well as towards individual women. It is increasingly unsatisfactory for each woman to negotiate for herself a way in. Those who appoint and promote have to acknowledge that women do not have to be like men and that what women bring to the workplace is of great value in its own terms.

At the moment there appears to be little encouragement for women to experiment with their different skills and talents or for men to show their more caring, intuitive and people-centred side. The rhetoric talks of 'caring, sharing management' but there is very little evidence to suggest that business, education and/or the market place have sufficiently changed in terms of language, values and ethics. Yet this is the very moment when management thinking has to be reassessed, in the light of world recession and when the old ways can be demonstrated not to have worked. Women may hold the key to the way forward, if those who hold power in organisations have the vision to empower them.

Some Tips

- it is difficult always to have trust in yourself, so find a mentor, a colleague or friend who will act as a sounding board for your ideas and actions
- try to be consistent – not a woman one day and 'one of the boys' the next

- accept that you are never going to be a full member of the boys' club because you will never be a man!
- do not accept that the way things are is the way they have to be.
- spend time talking and sharing with colleagues but do not end up as 'mummy'.

Notes

1. Loden, M., *Feminine Leadership and How to Succeed in Business Without Being One of the Boys*, Times Books, New York, 1985, p.4.
2. Richards, C., and Morgan, C., *Human Resource Management in Education,* OU Press, Milton Keynes, 1989, p.4.
3. Archer, J., and Lloyd, B., *Sex and Gender*, Penguin, Harmondsworth, 1982, p. 40.

4

Women Working with Women

'Be realistic: Plan for a miracle.'
Bhagwan Shree Rajneesh

Women co-workers can be a woman manager's very best and most loyal supporters. They can also have impossibly high expectations and some difficulties in dealing with woman to woman relationships which involve power. In this chapter we look at women working with women, in a whole range of different capacities and relationships.

Women are often perceived as having problems working with other women. We have all heard the stories about how bitchy an office full of women can be. Most of us have, at some stage in our career, come up against this problem in some form, yet in many all-female offices the workers are immensely supportive of each other. Women managers may, in understanding some of the tensions that come from working as women in an unfriendly environment, be able to build good working relationships and help other women overcome their reluctance to work with or suspicion of a woman boss.

It is possible, however, that on your climb up the career ladder you may have problems with certain women for a variety of reasons. Let us say right away that you will not have problems with all other women. Many will be very supportive and will give you all the help and backing they can. These are the people you need to befriend and, where possible, empower. A network of women friends you can trust gives you more power. The fact that you can talk over problems with them, ask their advice, share your success, will give you more confidence to 'go for it.'

Unfortunately, many women will be jealous of your success and that of others. Some will say they do not like working for a woman boss – we will look at some of the reasons later. It is far more difficult to pin down the different and often complex relationships a woman manager will have with other women than it is to look at the relationships between women.

Women as Managers – Good or Bad?

We would like to think that all women managers are good, but alas this is just not so. Many women managers are quite simply too nice! They worry about their self-image, how others see them. They want to be liked and respected by all. This can get in the way of a women manager's effectiveness. To be fair this is not a trait exhibited solely by women, we can think of many male managers with exactly the same problem.

Very often, being nice translates into not wanting to upset people by telling them the truth or talking about everything except the matter in hand. Far from making you well-liked, this irritates others who see you as a nice person, but completely unsuited for a management position. For the most part, people like to know where they stand and respect a manager far more for being firm on certain issues. Once you are a manager, respect is possibly more important than being liked by everyone. If you can achieve both, that is great – if not, settle for respect. On the other hand, be aware of the danger of emulating 'tough' male or female role models and ending up 'strong' and unsupportive and over-authoritative.

A woman manager needs to forget self-image and be herself. To be effective and get the job done well, she needs to set parameters to ensure others know exactly where they stand. That way there should be no misunderstandings. Today, it is generally acknowledged that all successful managers should exhibit the qualities usually credited to women, including an empathy with other people, openness in their dealings and the ability to communicate. Organisations are looking for facilitators. Women managers start off with a ready made advantage, but managing people is a lonely occupation. You may well find yourself with few real friends and this is why it is so important to keep your network of women friends.

Relationships with Women Managers—Allies or Enemies?

As women take their first steps on the career ladder, there is often an assumption that this minority group will be very close and help each other. Of course, this is not always the case. Some of our best friends will be other women managers but, equally, so will some of our toughest opponents.

Common Ground?

No matter what our relationship may be, we as managers, if not as women, have a great deal in common. As women managers we should have even more common ground. It is important that women managers focus on professional issues and not on clashing personalities. There will always be some people we do not like and some people who do not like us. This is as true of women as of men. Accepting this is important as it enables us to put any problems into perspective.

A woman manager working with other women who are often lower in the hierarchy can sometimes hit unexpected problems. Former colleagues, jealous of your success, may show this jealousy in many different ways. In some instances it can even go so far as the writing of vindictive letters to your superior, detailing every possible reason for not keeping you as a manager. In other cases they may try to ostracise you in some way that can make life very unpleasant. Others may look at you to change the world – usually immediately – 'now we have a woman boss things had better change. . .' and when that does not happen they turn on you. You are seen as not doing anything to help other women, as ensuring that other women do not get promotion, as changing your values as soon as you achieved managerial status and so on. How you dress and behave will be under scrutiny and you will not please everyone. This can mean that by the time you reach a senior management position you are almost totally isolated; yet another reason for holding on to your personal network of real friends for support.

To achieve common ground under these circumstances can be difficult, but in many instances small areas of agreement emerge and these provide the basis for future negotiation. Being adult and realistic about relationships allows us flexibility. People do have their prejudices and they can learn. It is always wise to allow a second chance and to work on the positive. Most people want to work in surroundings that are supportive and this is perhaps particularly true for many women. Thus, for example, sharing ownership of problems that have to be addressed and seeking help may allow those who have unrealistic views about you to get closer to you and to feel involved in joint solutions.

Often, we do not like to criticise other women managers openly. There is the feeling that 'we need to support each other, after all we're all in this together.' Unable or unwilling to offer constructive criticism, such comments become covert and simply give fuel to those who distrust women managers as a species. Sometimes, women managers can be obstructive, awkward and demanding. Maybe they feel threatened at work or are worried about something outside work. It does no harm to put yourself in their position and try to see their point of view. Maybe you can come to a compromise – after all our whole life is a compromise! Maybe other women managers need help or advice on problems they face. Often managers know they are not on top of their job and would welcome a friendly helping hand and good advice – as long as it is given in the spirit of friendship. There are times when everyone feels they have had enough. Too many people are prepared to criticise, not always constructively, and there are too few women in management positions for us to wish them harm.

Establishing Friendships – or not?

We have said that management is a lonely and often isolated existence. A woman in management will often find this problem magnified because of her gender. The higher up the career ladder a women manager climbs, the more isolated she becomes as she may well be the only woman in senior management. Women tend to gravitate towards other women managers in the workplace for support, and sometimes counselling. However, for a senior woman manager, it can be very difficult to turn to a junior for this friendship and support. It takes time to build trust, to find who is supportive and who is not, to find who will not repeat confidences and who is happy to help with advice. Yet out of this is often born friendship and maybe the start of a support network.

Women gravitating towards other women for support is fine and, as long as it is controlled, works well. Women managers may be great friends and allies but need to be careful that they are not labelled as a formidable team bound by gender rather than profession. This may be a cost you are willing and able to pay for your networks and support, but you should be aware of the risk. In other ways, of course, unity is strength.

Breaking up Is Hard to Do!

What happens when close friends disagree and a rift

develops? This can be horrendous in the workplace and may be more difficult for women managers who probably have fewer friends at work to start with. If this should happen it is important that you endeavour to sort out any differences. Never resort to sulking, bitching or a 'dirty tricks' campaign, as you can be sure that, as women managers, your credibility will drop to zero or below. It can be very difficult, if not impossible, to recover completely from a blow of that magnitude. Women managers should remember that people have long memories when it comes to problems with women in management positions. It is amazing how much shorter their memories appear when things run smoothly. Try applying your management skills to rescue unpleasant situations and remember – it is never good to lose a friend.

A Kindred Spirit?

The support of fellow women managers is second to none when it is working well. They will have a knowledge of the problems you face and the circumstances you are in. They can be a source of strength and inspiration. They will often rally to help when the going gets tough. Women managers who do not work with you are often great friends to have, and their views of your work problems can be more objective than your own as they are not so close to the problem. Their experiences enrich your knowledge. There is no threat or fear in a relationship with women managers outside your company and there is a great deal to gain. Our book-writing venture has been for us a very practical demonstration of that.

Finding and/or establishing a network cannot always be easy, but keep a look out for networks and clubs you can join. They may appear in professional journals, be mentioned at professional conferences or be spoken of in business communications. Remember, a smile and a friendly word will get you into a dialogue with someone who may become a great friend and ally in the future.

Relationships with Women Subordinates – Mentor or Spy?

Women managers often form close and successful relationships with their subordinates, particularly as mentors. Close and intimate working practices can develop with the emphasis on not letting one another down. This is where the relationship is at its best. Unfortunately there is a flip side to this particular coin and when the relationship is not healthy there can be great problems. Subordinates are ideally placed to undermine their superior and to highlight and expose their shortcomings. This, of course, is not exclusive to the female but, given a woman's power of influencing, could be seriously damaging. The woman manager scores with her subordinates because she has understanding. She has usually had, or even still has, the same problems they face and that gives her a distinct advantage. She is able to relate to them in a way few male managers are able to do.

Listening to staff's frustrations is usually the starting point, having created the environment to encourage them to 'come clean.' A woman manager's best counselling skills are needed here, as well as a commitment to develop her subordinates to the limit. A word of warning. Beware of trying to live your life again and fulfil your dreams through them if it is not commensurate with their agenda. The sacrifices you have made may not be entertained by them, whatever their ability.

Taking account of a woman subordinate's circumstances and ensuring that these can be facilitated whilst meeting an organisation's goals can sometimes seem an impossible dream. You will need to bring all your creative thinking and tactical solution-devising skills into play. A satisfied subordinate will see you as a magician and her motivation level will soar. You need to watch for the signals that all is not well and help remove the barriers as far as you are able.

A woman manager can expect to have criticism levelled at her if she treats a female member of the team more favourably than the males. This is just as bad as women being treated unfavourably compared to men. It is sometimes easier to strike up a relationship with another woman, but being seen to be fair is an important element of management.

Some of your women subordinates may wish to infer that your relationship is closer than in fact it is. Information you give in trust could be used against you. Someone who knows what colour your bath towels are may choose to drop this in conversation to suggest they are regular visitors to your home. This, together with their promotion or their being allocated 'plum' tasks, could build up an entirely distorted picture. Moreover, a picture is difficult to disprove. You will never stop people making up information if they are so inclined, but you should work to eliminate or limit the damage.

We can think of instances that lead us to believe that relationships can become more difficult the higher up the career ladder you climb. You may be more fearful as a manager that your friendship might be exploited and you do see the world of work through different eyes. As your responsibility and decision making powers grow, the more distant and mistrusting your female subordinates may become. They may try forcing you to focus on minor details rather than the strategic issues that are important to the direction of the business. It is all too easy to be side-tracked in the name of friendship. You need to share with your colleagues the direction you are taking and the overview of the business that you need to be aware of in your new position.

Nothing can compare, however, to a successful mentoring relationship when a woman manager supports and helps a subordinate into management. This should be, and often is, the basis of a successful supporting friendship and network. Mentoring works the other way, too. Why not ask your secretary or clerk to show you how to do certain things you may not be so good at? They will gain as much in confidence and morale as you will gain in knowledge.

The Secretary – Friend or Foe?

As a woman manager, you are quite likely to have the luxury of a secretary or personal assistant. A good secretary is a blessing and, all too often, a rarity. She (or nowadays he) can think like you, plan like you, anticipate the support you need and gauge how you are likely to react in any given situation. This telepathy seems to be at its strongest when the secretary and manager are both women. The woman manager usually understands, or at least tries to understand, how her secretary feels and values her professionalism. The relationship is often frank yet business-like. There is often a warm 'looking out for each other' side to the relationship. There is a high degree of mutual respect for one another's strengths and weaknesses and this close team-work can be joyous to observe. The woman manager and her secretary can be the best mentors for each other.

Of course, the aspersions cast on a male manager who asks his secretary to accompany him on a business trip do not exist for the woman manager, unless she has a male secretary! The opportunity to enrich her secretary's job and provide personal development is easier in the all-female relationship. This can be a real advantage for a secretary, enabling her to perform better, achieve greater job satisfaction and gain promotion.

The down side for some secretaries is that this close relationship, together with a female manager, prevents them from using their manipulative powers. Some female secretaries like to 'get round' their bosses and they find it difficult to do this with a woman boss. One secretary told us, 'I used to be able to manipulate my last boss. I could twist him round my little finger. I can't do that to my female boss – she'd know what I was doing!'

A bad secretary (or a badly-managed secretary)is,

on the other hand, a tyrant. The secretary acts as an information filter for her manager. A bad secretary may choose to filter too much, leaving her manager completely in the dark. She screens telephone calls and often manages to exclude or put off an important colleague or client. She may 'accidentally forget' to pass on messages or, even worse, she may pass on an extremely distorted version. She is also in possession of confidential information which may be dynamite if she is indiscreet.

We all have 'off' days, but when the bad secretary is having one we are walking on eggshells. Worse still, when you see the moody look on her face in the morning you know you are in for a rough time. Sulking, together with playing guessing games as to why she is acting as she is, are the bane of the woman manager's life when dealing with a bad secretary. It becomes an uphill task, as you can spend as much time sorting your secretary out as you spend on the work you are paid to do!

Fortunately, most women managers have a professional and pleasurable relationship with their secretary. She is regarded as an important, valuable management asset. Being open with her, trusting her and encouraging her will pay dividends for you.

The good boss-secretary relationship offers the woman manager special STRENGTHS; she can save you time, be your guardian angel to protect you from the world, and be your friend and representative. There are potential WEAKNESSES; she can fail to give you accurate information, try to dominate you and take a lot of your time. There are OPPORTUNITIES to be her mentor and supporter. You may be training a future manager! The THREATS are related to indiscretion, dishonesty and an ability to do your reputation great harm. All these factors need to be balanced and carefully watched.

Career Paths

Finding the correct career path, or switching career paths if you feel you want to change career, is not easy, as many women have found to their cost. Unfortunately, we tend to start work without any real idea of where we want to be in 15 to 20 years' time, other than 'in management'. Yet our first job can signal the end of our chances.

In 1990 the Institute of Manpower Studies released reports which stated that women make early career choices which restrict their chances of obtaining senior management positions. Women traditionally have found their forte working in marketing, public relations, personnel, and administration, all areas where they can utilise their special skills. However the report stated that these areas are seen as support sectors or support functions. Directors and senior managers believe that it is very difficult, just working in these support areas, to obtain the wide 'business experience' they see as necessary for senior management positions. They may not be correct, but we have been warned!

There are still barriers to be overcome in terms of career paths and that is obviously one major hurdle. One of the largest hurdles, however, is that of perception. People have a perception of some jobs being 'male' and some 'female'. Ask yourself what comes into your mind when you hear the terms nurse, engineer, pilot, secretary; frightening isn't it? One thing is sure, young women need to decide where they want to go in their career very early on, in order to give themselves the best possible chance of obtaining their objective.

To be fair, times are changing and many more women managers are involved in engineering, manufacturing and other traditionally 'male' occupations. What has obviously changed very little is that many predominantly 'female' jobs have no obvious upwards career path. Where does the good secretary go if she wants promotion? She may become a PA, but she will find it very difficult to move out of the secretarial area unless she works for an employer such as the BBC that has a reputation for its former secretaries becoming programme producers and editors.

We know a few female graduates who have taken a year's secretarial course on graduation. They then obtain jobs as secretaries and hope to become managers in years to comes. A fortunate few may make it but it will be difficult. Yet secretaries and PAs could be the managers of the future. They work closely with their own managers. They are often left to run everything virtually single-handed and in many cases have a large say in the decision-making. They see where things have gone wrong and why. They have first-hand experience of management.

Changing career mid-stream to give yourself better management opportunities is not easy. Many employers look askance at any women attempting to do this and immediately fall back on the 'you have no relevant experience' routine. Some are sympathetic, but would still not appoint you. If you feel you need to change the direction in which you are heading, you need to stop and consider. It may help if you look for something compatible with your skills or related to interests you have outside work.

Would training help? If so, you can go on various courses (even if you have to go in the evening) in order to broaden your experience and learn other skills. Once you have helped yourself in this way, you may find an approach to your present employer is sensible. They know what you are capable of and the fact that you have been prepared to learn new skills will be a definite plus. Your present employer would not be taking such a large risk as would a new employer. Many women have found this works and are now on the management ladder.

Sometimes you may be held back because your qualifications are higher than those of your superior. This can be difficult, but a word with personnel, explaining that you wish to make your career with the company and could they please consider you for anything suitable, will often do the trick.

At other times you may get impatient because you have been on the same rung of the career ladder for what, to you at least, seems eternity! You may be quite happy in your work but cannot wait to move on upwards. This is where you need to pause awhile. If you have reached a senior management position, you will know there are less jobs available for you now, after all the pyramid gets narrower at the top. Companies have very definite views on people in senior management. If you move, constantly looking for promotion, you are seen as never finishing what you have started, yet if you stay for too long in one position you are seen as lacking ambition. As you cannot win whatever you do, it would seem sensible to review your position! Have you built up a supportive network? Have you friends within your organisation who can be relied upon? Are you beginning to find you are not so isolated? Just remember that if you move on you will have to start again. Unless you are convinced you will get no further with your present employer, it may make more sense to stay. After all, supportive friends and networks help your powerbase.

What is important is that whatever career you have chosen, you keep on moving constantly upwards. There will be times when progress is slow and other times when you move so quickly that you feel completely lost. If you feel you are in the wrong career to reach your goal, do something about it. Who knows, you may end up at the very top.

Increasingly, whatever your chosen career path, you will be likely to work with a woman boss, or meet women on your way up. New ways of relating do need to be negotiated, as does so much else of the manager's life. Resist the temptation to ignore women or to take their criticism too much to heart. It is important to learn who to trust and when to listen. We are still in pioneering days and women at the top need all the help they can get. In giving this, or in helping other women climb, we help not just get the statistical balance right, but also allow both men and women to build new ways of working.

5

How do I Manage the Boundaries?

'Had we but world enough and time . . .'
Andrew Marvell

For many working women, this is the area which is at the hub of their lives and concerns. In planning this section, we certainly were able to share a number of worries which impinged not only on our working but also our personal lives. For many of the questions raised here there are no answers, yet it is clear that any woman on a fast career track has to face many of these issues and have speedy and effective survival strategies. In this chapter we look at those areas where work and our other lives overlap and we try to face up to some of the contradictions and problems.

Identifying the Twilight Zones

We agreed that there are a number of areas which fall clearly into that twilight zone we describe and all of which caused us anxiety at times. These include expectations that managers will, for example:

- attend business social events, like dinners, lunches, working breakfasts and drinks sessions

- undertake business travel, usually alone, rarely in the company of other women and involving long car journeys, overnight stays and travel outside of the UK
- cope with the existence at work of a past or present partnership with a male colleague where the world appears to be watching and listening
- handle friendships with men and women which spill outside the boundaries of work
- make enough and proper space for personal leisure and relaxation
- deal with issues of health and stress and maintain peace of mind
- balance home and work demands, personal inclinations and the pull of duty.

This list, like all the lists in this book, is merely indicative. We believe it to be important that women rising in their careers and facing ever more of these issues identify their own list, preferably in writing. It is crucial that we are honest with ourselves and recognise the tensions. Facing up to them and the inherent and often insoluble contradictions can be helpful in itself. Instead of blaming ourselves, we can see our daily management of these and the difficult choices we make within a context. We can review the list regularly and will find that some worries, like travelling alone, for example, can drop lower down the list with experience, whilst new issues of families or friends may rise. We do need to congratulate ourselves on successes and to make sure that we make enough 'selfish' choices.

Issues of Conscience

We all feel that there are areas where personal concerns and personal morality become tested in the work place. A relationship or friendship might be an example of this where, for example, a senior manager might be put in a difficult position, particularly as a woman, if she has friends lower down or rising up the organisation. Similarly, a woman who is opening and trusting in her personal relationships may have to modify her behaviour if she is dealing with people who will attempt to manipulate her. As a professional, she will know or learn the difference, but the experience can affect her social behaviour and personal expectations.

The aim is that we become comfortable with ourselves as people whose careers are a significant part of their lives. Therefore it is important, we feel, to find one or more people in similar positions to share these worries with. They will probably be women, since admitting fear or failure seems to come harder and to send a different message to many men. It is perhaps helpful to have confidants outside your workplace and here the various women's professional networks are invaluable. If you can not find one that suits you, start one! Get a few professional women together for lunch in a local restaurant and the support and shared concerns which emerge may surprise you. Notwithstanding all the jealousies and false expectations we have of each other, women, often with quite disparate backgrounds, tend to communicate quickly and honestly with each other on matters like this. This may be a feature of the stage we are at as aspirant women; once more of us have power this shared understanding of what it is like to be excluded from power may go. Let us hope that it doesn't and use it while it is current!

We are aware that in some circles it is taboo to discuss fears. The 'it's not a problem just a new opportunity' cult which permeates our business language can make some women fear that their concerns indicate, either to themselves or others, that they are not 'up to it.' As women, we all juggle a wide range of expectations and responsibilities that society places on us, from the care of the young and elderly to the responsibility to manage work and home life.

Whose Time Is It Anyway?

Time is at the centre of our practical and emotional problems, we feel. Women's time has always been undervalued by society; the woman who raises children and keeps home is described as 'unemployed.' We often do those things as well as follow a career and those women without the responsibility (and support) of a partner or children, still have a network of family and friends to care for. The everyday tasks of the maintenance of the fabric of our homes and lives thus fills the spare places left over from work. Rarely, if time has to be 'found' for such work, does it come out of our working timetable, it is much more likely that we erode that little but essential space we keep for ourselves as individuals. We are asking throughout this chapter whether we do have to be different women at work and at home or play. If we do, then we need to be clear about and protect the boundaries and, if not, then we need to be sure that one part of our life does not spoil the others for us.

Into the Twilight Zone

Within an organisation, women are often seen to have a useful role to play, especially at senior levels, in helping to manage business entertaining and public relations events smoothly. Not only is it useful to show that this is a forward-looking company and has its woman on the board, but women's years of experience as daughters, sisters and wives in the domestic sphere make them good at making people feel comfortable and at ease. Undoubtedly many women do have skills in this arena and we suggest that, whilst avoiding the trap of becoming invisible behind the coffee pot, we can use our social skills to the advantage of our careers and our companies.

A simple and practical question which arises at the first mention of such occasions is 'what shall I wear?' The question is not trivial, for we will be noticed and we will be judged. It is not fair, but that is how it works! Thus whilst we can learn the 'suits mean power' code for the daytime and recognise that dark and formal is required for interviews or presentations, in social situations there are few rules to follow. Most importantly, you need to feel comfortable and not dressed in a style which is totally alien to your view of yourself. Women can break the rules on dress, but carefully and within strict limits and nowhere is the path more treacherous than at social events. Avoid the cleavage and long hair, be careful with junk jewellery and make sure that your clothes tell others who you are. One solution is the suit with a 'softer' top and some different jewellery. We each develop a repertoire of our own and there are few rules which apply universally.Most of these are common sense; ignore them only with great care and an awareness of what you are saying in yet another kind of language.

Almost always, social events at work run on from the daily routine and we face them tired and jaded. This is the time for careful planning, perhaps for an hour at the nearest leisure centre and a chance to refresh. Do not try to fit in shopping or cooking the kids' tea as well; this is work and you need to be as prepared as you would be for a meeting. Keep a few rules for yourself; eat little, drink even less and have your business cards ready.

Overnight Stays and Conferences

Much the same advice applies when you stay away from home for a training course or conference. Not only do you have to be prepared yourself, but you also have to ensure that the ranch back home can function without you. This invariably means you have to spend time writing lists for everyone, organising lifts for children, shopping and planning well in advance.

One woman we know, who stays away a great deal, programmes, with alarms, a Psion Organiser. The alarms are set for important times such as the time to get up, take Laura to Brownies and put milk bottles out. With the alarm, the appropriate message flashes continuously across the screen. You may well think this is going too far, but it works for her!

Once at the conference, do remember to enjoy it. There is no point in worrying over what might be going on at home. You need to concentrate 100% on the course. It is amazing how we tend to forget all about pressures of home and work while we are away. This is why so many conferences and training courses are held in hotels. It ensures that participants are in a completely different environment and able to leave their problems behind. While you are being waited on hand and foot, do not feel guilty. If you are a mother, you are experiencing no better service than your family has from you nearly every day!

There may be occasions when you find yourself the 'token woman'. This has happened to nearly all of us at some time and can be turned to our advantage. Whilst we are unlikely to remember every other person at the conference or training course, we can rest assured that most delegates there will certainly remember us, simply because of our rarity value.

If you have attended a conference, on your return send a summary of the main points to your boss and anyone else you think may have an interest. This is one way of ensuring that you get noticed. Harvey Coleman of IBM has researched the factors that affect promotion. He found that 10% depends on your past performance, 30% on having a successful image and 60% on whether people in your organisation know you or not! Make sure you also follow up contacts you have made with a brief letter or some relevant documentation. If the contact is with another woman, you can suggest meeting for lunch, but that is clearly more sensitive in the case of a male contact. It becomes even more important in this case that you sent the right signals at the conference, by your dress and behaviour.

The Workaholic

Sometimes our work keeps us away from home more than we would like. This affects both the single woman and the woman with a partner and/or children. A single woman may find it impossible to form meaningful relationships when she is constantly at work or jetting off to distant places. Friendships are affected, even long-standing friendships are difficult to keep up when you can rarely meet. It is also difficult to relax and keep work in perspective.

For the woman who has a partner and/or children, there are a different set of difficulties. Many men arrive home late from work each night and work weekends. For the most part, they have a partner to keep everything running. What happens when both partners have the same problem, or it is the woman who is constantly working? Invariably it is the female partner who bends a little. Remember that a partnership is a two-way relationship and it should not always be the same partner giving way.

It is too easy to find ourselves absorbed in our work, especially if have a job we really enjoy. There is nothing wrong in finding fulfilment in our careers, but we need to be aware of that thin dividing line between being a workaholic and being a hard worker. Remember there has to be time for relaxation to recharge the batteries. No one can keep going day after day with no real rest without suffering the consequences. If you have no alternative but to be away from home more than you are 'in residence', it is even more important that time is set aside regularly for partners, children, friends and, let us not forget, self.

Friends

One of the major problems for a woman manager is friendship. Friendships outside work may be neglected due to pressures of work and friendships at work can be problematic. At work, as a manager, it can be very difficult to strike up friendships. As you rise higher up the managerial ladder, it becomes difficult to keep friendships made at work. If you leave for another position, you probably know no one there and you may be the only woman on that level of management. In other words – life at the top can be lonely.

Friends made before your rise in status may feel uncomfortable if you try to continue the friendship. Jealousy or envy may be involved. Some friends may not understand how you obtained promotion because they had never thought of you as a manager. The woman manager too will change. Suddenly it is no longer 'them and us'; you are now 'one of them'. Old friends may expect you to pass on gossip or news they would not otherwise get to hear. You, on the other hand, will be conscious that there are certain things you should not pass on. Thus friendships are strained as they believe you think you are now too good for them, whilst you would dearly love to still be involved but cannot.

Let us look at friendship, especially within the workplace.

- once you are in a management position, you become a role model for others who aspire
- once you are a manager, others in the organisation have certain expectations of you. So, you are not expected to complain about your lot, nor show temper or any other form of emotion. Who can you turn to? If you have not already lost them – your friends out of work, or your partner.

You may now be in a position where you can help other women to attain managerial status. On your rise 'through the ranks', you will have seen people you consider worth promoting. Maybe you think they have not been encouraged, or they need more training in certain areas. There is no reason why you should not make suggestions to them or ask them to take a meeting for you, for example, to gain experience. This is a practical way of empowering others. Nothing gives more pleasure than seeing someone you have encouraged and helped get their feet on the managerial ladder.

Too few women are in positions where they can empower others. For example, whilst 60% of teachers are women, only 5% of women are heads and deputies. To make matters worse, men are 50% more likely to be given job-related training by their employers. It is vitally important, therefore, that those of us who are in a position of empowerment ensure that we do all we can.

There are problems. Some women will abuse the process and assume that they have an automatic right to promotion merely because the manager/director/

administrator is a woman. They may be abusive when they are constantly passed over for the very simple reason that they are not good enough. Some will take it on themselves to gossip about the woman manager, or write complaints about her. It then looks as though she is unable to control or manage her staff! Of course, were it a male manager involved, the problem would no doubt be seen in a different light. The well-known saying that 'a woman needs to be twice as good as a man doing the same job to get on' stills tends to hold true.

Morality

Once more we enter a twilight area. We have talked about 'using' situations to our advantage. Is it legitimate to use a person in this way? What if you feel you are being used? There are a range of issues which need to be addressed as we look at this aspect of our practice and experience.

We need to be aware of the problems that can arise through our personal views on morality and ethics. This is yet another area where many people would argue that women's views tend to be different from those of the average male. It is not easy to avoid moral and ethical issues. No matter how liberal our views may be, there will always be a point at which we say, 'enough.' A woman manager may have great problems reconciling her own personal moral and ethical views with those of her employers and/or boss. The occasion may even arise when it is a case of job versus personal ethics. In that case, which do you choose?

All too often we come down on the side of the

company because to do otherwise would cost us our job. It can be extremely difficult to find alternative employment once you have left a position due to 'a difference of opinion.' It immediately brands you as a trouble-maker. The newspapers often have stories of directors who have perpetrated fraud or other criminal acts for many years. In most cases their managers must have some knowledge of these activities, yet they choose not to report them because they feel they have too much to lose. How we feel about our job and ourselves as individuals is important. If we find it difficult to live with ourselves because we have compromised our beliefs, then we have real problems. It is important, wherever possible, to stand firm. The ethics that are the norm within an organisation will vary according to the company culture. Unfortunately, this cannot be assessed easily at a job interview and it may be some time before you realise that it is not in tune with your own views.

Some companies are well-known for the benevolent way they treat their staff. Alongside stories of caring employers, we read of instances where companies go out of their way to terminate the employment of a woman who is pregnant, using all kinds of excuses. How would you feel if you worked for this type of employer? You may well hold very different ethical and moral views to those of your employer, yet work quite happily for them because your particular job does not bring you into direct conflict. On the other hand, you may find yourself employed in an area where conflict is inevitable. It is one thing to hold certain moral and ethical views and entirely another to always uphold them in everyday business.

A survey of 1000 executives showed that nearly 25% believe that ethical standards can impede successful careers. 68% admit that younger managers are driven to compromise their ethics 'by the desire for wealth and material things.'[1] Subsequently, Human Resource managers who were surveyed said the people most likely to be unethical are the middle managers in the 40–45 age group who are driven by the desire to 'make it before it's too late.' The next group most likely to be unethical are top managers who tell subordinates to 'do whatever you have to do, just don't tell me about it'.[2]

You may well have heard something similar yourself. It is very difficult to make a stand when unethical behaviour is the norm, often made worse because the woman manager may well be the 'token woman.' A major problem for women managers is that too often their views on morality or ethics are seen as an emotional response rather than a rational statement.

Other issues in this area may be more personal. Your own values will affect the way you behave in given situations. These values within working relationships are very important. They affect the way others see us and the way we handle different situations.

Missed Messages

It is generally acknowledged that women express themselves differently to men. Thus where a woman manager may say one thing, her male colleague may get an entirely different message. When a Judge in a recent rape case stated that 'When a woman says No she often means Yes', he was expressing one of the most dangerous and irresponsible stereotypes about women. As this stands, inexcusably, we might say, at one end of the spectrum of misunderstanding, more subtle confusions stand at the other end. Women, despite all the jokes to the contrary, are often direct and to the point. The problem is that we are not seen in that light. People hear what they want to hear.

Ideas' Thieves

How often have you come up with a really good idea and seen someone else claim it as theirs? The trouble is that many women lack confidence in their own ability. They may not put their idea forward and someone else will think of it in time or they talk about it to all and sundry, which enables an 'ideas' thief' to run with it. Ideas' thieves are one of the most annoying species we know. One problem is that women are often far too trusting. They tend to talk to others about their ideas, which gives someone the opportunity to pick up the idea and pass it off as their own. It is not just women who fall prey to ideas' thieves, men too have problems. ideas' thieves can be either sex.

This is an important issue, because the people with the ideas get noticed and the people who get noticed are in the frame for promotions. Therefore it is vital to prevent it happening to you.

Some suggestions:

● do not discuss your ideas with anyone you do not trust absolutely

- have confidence in your own ability. After all, you had the idea in the first place. Why should it not be a good one?
- write your idea down and pass it on to the appropriate person – keeping a copy. This way the origin is known. You may want to bring your idea up in a meeting if you have the opportunity. Do not sit there and wait for too long, someone else may be thinking along similar lines. Make your suggestion at the first available opportunity
- your idea may seem so blindingly obvious that you cannot believe it is legitimate. Remember, this may be the very reason no one has thought about it! It is too obvious.

It is, of course, not always this easy. Sometimes you may find that you have implemented changes and find other people taking the credit. It does no harm to be assertive and let everyone know that you were the architect of the changes. Let the ideas' thief know too. After a while they may turn their attention to someone else who will not make a fuss.

Overall, the message of this chapter is that, as a professional woman, you must value yourself and not be ashamed to put your views and your needs first. If, when driving a car, you give a lot of attention to your passengers' comfort, you will give less to your driving and thus the safety of everyone in the car. Caring for others who are important to us, and doing a job well, even with great passion, can only be successfully achieved if we are taking care of ourselves at the centre of this, our world.

Notes

1. Schellhardt, T. D., 'What Bosses Think About Corporate Ethics', in *Wall Street Journal*, April 16, 1988.
2. Plawin, D., and Blum, A., 'The Young and Ruthless', in *Changing Times*, August, 1988.

6

Is It All Worth It?

'Too much of a good thing can be wonderful.'
Mae West

Throughout this book, we have attempted to look at the various issues that concern the woman manager. No doubt you can identify with many of the situations we have described. Now we come to the million dollar question . . . . is it all worth it? Most of us ask this question more than once in our careers and the answer is usually a qualified 'yes.'

In this chapter we look at the variety of balancing acts performed by all women who choose to have a career outside the home. This balancing act is performed both in the home and outside. Women who choose not to have a career still have to balance different aspects of their life. If they choose to pursue a career as well, the challenges are even greater.

If the different components can be balanced successfully, all will be well. Too often there are so many balls in the air at the same time that, inevitably, some are in danger of falling to the ground. The costs can be great and there is a feeling of guilt over small things left undone, regardless of the reason. How many of us have had to choose between staying at work to finish off a job properly or leaving the job half-finished in order to attend our child's school play or our partner's office 'do'?

Too High a Cost?

In this chapter we will be looking more closely at the costs involved in pursuing careers. These are not simply financial, as in the case of childcare or housecare, but also emotional, affecting relationships including those with partners, family, friends and colleagues. On the other hand, there are opportunities for an improved standard of living and the feelings of self-fulfilment and job satisfaction that we may not attain in any other way.

Guilty or Not Guilty?

We turn then to the question of guilt and how it can be dealt with effectively. It is in a woman's make-up to feel guilty over anything she feels remotely responsible for: missed anniversaries, missed appointments, forgetting to sympathise or congratulate someone and even employing a cleaner rather than cleaning the house herself! Are we unusual in this? Do men suffer these feelings of guilt too? The evidence suggests not.

Pulled Two Ways?

From feelings of guilt, it is a short step to looking at our careers and how they affect our families and friends. After all, outside work there is a 'real life' to be lived and expectations at that level are far different to those of work. How many 'levels' is a woman manager expected to cope with and how is the balancing act performed successfully?

What is Most Important?

We next look at the one way women do manage to cope – by juggling their time, often at great cost. Most women who have careers outside the home soon learn time-management skills from experience, otherwise life would become impossible. How can we arrange our time effectively with so many competing factors? There is no single answer as different women will have different ideas on the relative importance of the same issues. However, all women managers have constantly to juggle their time to fit in with other people both at work and at home.

Sit Back and Consider?

Sometimes we have to let go and let others cope for themselves while we take a back seat. This is never very easy, but is essential for our well-being. There are also times when a woman needs to let out her pent-up feelings and talk things over so that problems can be talked through and seen rationally. This may be to her partner, a member of the family or a good friend she can trust and who will understand. At the end of the day, only you will know whether it has all been worth it or not.

The Story so Far

Women who choose to work and take on responsible positions as well as having a family have been assailed on all sides in the past few years by the media. There have been headlines berating working mothers for breeding a generation of 'latch-key kids' or, even worse, leaving their children to roam the streets until such time as they or their partner returned home from work. Statistics have been produced to show that this lack of parental (for parental read 'mother's'!) attention caused their children to take to a life of vandalism and crime. All of a sudden, working mothers were made out to be uncaring, anti-social women who could not be bothered to look after their own children. The debate raged for some time and many women must have experienced feelings of guilt as the 'experts' told them how they were damaging their children's chances in life.

However another point of view comes from Patricia Pollock, managing editor of a publishing department at the Meredith Corporation in America:

> 'I've also learned a lot from raising children. I spent a lot of time with the kids trying to solve all their problems for them, and along the way I realised that this was not what I was supposed to do. I learned to create an atmosphere so they could learn how to cope with a problem and solve it themselves . . . In the same way, as a manager, I don't believe in being the provider of answers – people need to learn on their own. This turns out to be trusting people.'[1]

Now the wheel has turned full circle with the media telling the government how important it is to provide nursery facilities to enable more women to safely and cheaply leave their children so they can take up or continue their careers. The government is encouraging schools to be left open until early evening and during school holidays to assist the working mother. Employers are given tax incentives to run creches for employees. What has brought about this change of heart? A change in expert opinions? Outrage from mothers? No, quite simply the experts discovered that the UK workforce, in a few years time, will not be large enough to keep the economy moving without many more women working!

This means that more and more women will be performing those balancing acts which are so essential when time is divided between home and work.

Swings and Roundabouts

Let us start by looking at the costs, not merely in terms of money, that the aspiring woman manager has to meet. To balance these we will also examine the benefits that we feel we can attain.

Undoubtedly, a major factor in a woman's life is her domestic circumstances. Whether she is married, or has a partner, whether she has children or remains single, will influence both her career and her views about her life.

Different Lives, Different Women

Singledom

If the woman manager, for what ever reason, remains single, she benefits by being able to apply herself wholeheartedly to her career. She has no need to worry about going away for long periods of time, or working late nearly every night. There is no partner to consider. However there are costs; no-one to talk things over with in the evening, the loneliness of the empty house or flat, no-one to share the triumphs with as well as the lows. Very often the single woman manager has only 'work' to keep her occupied, since the temptation, given the freedom, to spend a great deal of time doing a job which is satisfying and enjoyable is very strong. Thus she works late at the office, takes work home and will even give up her weekends to work. Her job becomes all consuming and the friends and hobbies she has may slip into second place with an assumption that 'one day' there will be time for them. New relationships have to be negotiated through these difficult waters and her partner must be someone who can understand her commitment to work. The successful and powerful woman, sure of her own path and in control of her own life, can be a frightening prospect and thus relation-ships are rarely smooth. Her partner may have his or her own commitment to work and they can end up competing in a number of ways. On the other hand, the single woman has her career, her own income, her skills, her successes and her contacts, some of whom will become friends. No-one can afford to let the scales swing entirely to the side of work; balance is essential for all of us. The single career woman needs to be aware of how seductive it is to neglect leisure and friendships in the cause of work.

Coupledom

If she decides to marry should she marry, early on in her career or later when she is better established? Research, with the benefit of hindsight, has shown that this often depends on the type of partner chosen and the attitude of the employing company. Unfortunately, unless a previous woman manager has trodden the same path before, the company's response is an unknown factor. Neither do we always look at prospective partners with an eye to them being ideal for our career prospects! Whatever happened to love! There are costs and benefits associated with both choices but only the person involved can decide which, on balance, is best for her.

To Have or not to Have – Children

The decision over taking a partner is nothing compared to that of whether or not to have children, and when. If a decision is made to have children sooner rather than later, the woman manager can pick up her career again, but may find it difficult to really get herself established back on the career track. If children come along later, she is often more established at work and may feel her career less threatened although her employer may think differently.

However, there is no hard and fast rule. Some women find that having children gives them a different per-spective on life and they suddenly find their career shooting ahead. Others choose to slow down their career aspirations for a time. An uproar was caused recently in America over the proposal that companies introduce a 'Mommy Track' for women willing to slow down their careers for a time while they are bringing up children. Many women felt strongly that companies should adapt their working structures and practices to suit the needs of their employees, including mothers, rather than the other way round. The debate continues.

Most careers have ups and downs, quite naturally, and it is often difficult to decide whether any set-backs are due to having a family or not. Several women have said how having children has helped them to 'switch off' from work once they arrive home. 'It's therapeutic,' said one television executive, 'I now feel I have something to come home for. I don't have time to worry about work. I give myself absolutely to the family when I'm home and they tire me out to such an extent that I now sleep better than I ever have before!'

Nevertheless, it is never easy once children are on the scene regardless of the mother's age. Many women feel employers take them less seriously once there are children involved. It is assumed that the woman manager with children will no longer wish or be able to work late, take on special responsibilities, work away from home (even for a day), attend functions after work or be sent on training courses away from home. In some instances this may be the case but cannot be taken as a blanket assumption. Invariably when this happens, the woman manager starts to lose out on opportunities because she is not seen to be at certain events and has not done the necessary training for promotion.

It can be difficult to get across to male managers that you are quite happy to go away if necessary and have no objection, if it is urgent, to working late occasionally, as long as you have the opportunity to arrange for someone to look after the children. Many men would see this as a dereliction of duty on your part and wonder about any woman who put her work before her children.

However, do remember that most women who have children would not like to be without them and many who wish to do continue to pursue successful careers and have busy and fulfilled lives. You just need to be aware that other people's perception of you and your abilities may change for a time!

Once children arrive, there is another decision to be made, that of part-time or full-time work. Will credibility be lost if you decide on part-time or maybe job-share? That you have children who take up your time is rather more obvious to everyone if the part-time route is chosen and will, for the most part, be seen as a decision to give up the career path for a time.

With an increase in divorce and second marriages, some women 'inherit' children. This can be more difficult, depending on the child's age, as there may well be problems of acceptance. Each case is different and only you will know how best to cope and whether your career goes on the 'back-burner' for a while. Unfortunately, there are still very few 'job-share' opportunities available, although some employers will agree to it if asked. This is one way of keeping your hand in at work and still being able to spend more time at home with your children.

If the children's father lives with the family then there is someone to share the responsibilities with.

Many men are taking a much greater role in bringing up their children. After all, if you are both holding down responsible jobs it is only right that the load be shared equally.

Research on senior women managers has shown that they tend to be single or childless. Where there are children, they tend to have fewer than average and have them later in life. A survey of 1500 women managers showed that 30% felt their careers had been helped by having family responsibilities, 30% indicated their careers had been harmed and 40% felt it had made no difference.[2]

The British Institute of Management says that 93% of its male membership is married, but only 58% of its women are and in America, 90% of male executives have children by the age of 40, while only 35% of women executives do.[3] Also, whilst a marriage and children is seen as a definite asset for a male manager, showing that he has a sense of responsibility and stability, it is frequently seen as a liability for a woman.

Dr Dee Soda[4], a New York psychologist, tells us:

'The difficult thing women have to recognise is that they cannot have it all – you have to make choices. Are you going to have a family now and leave a career until later? Are you going to have a child this year or next year? Or in some cases are you going to get married or not at all?'

Amazing isn't it, that no-one talks of men having to make these choices. In fact, a woman needs to recognise that very often her aspirations cannot be met simultaneously, but they may all be capable of being achieved over a period of time.

Motherhood or Parenthood?

We have argued that more men are taking a larger role in bringing up their children but, nevertheless, the care of children is still seen as very much the responsibility of the mother. She is seen as the natural person to look after the children, especially at the pre-school stage. Should she wish to continue full-time employment, the provision of child care is often seen as her problem.

This brings us to the monetary costs associated with having a family – the costs of childcare and the lack of suitable childcare facilities. If employers are successfully to use women as a means of combating the forecast labour shortage, they need to supply more flexible working methods and hours and better child care arrangements such as workplace nurseries. Governments also need to consider more local authority nurseries and tax incentives. A recent report published by the Institute of Manpower Studies said:

> 'The UK has the worst childcare provisions and parental provisions (including maternity leave schemes) in Europe, with only 1.3% of under fives having a nursery place.'

Two years later there was no change. Cooper and Davidson in *Shattering the Glass Ceiling*[6] illustrate this:

> 'Less than 1 in 5000 women workers can use

nurseries provided by their employers and only 1 in 20,000 gets a childcare allowance from the firm. In addition, fewer than 2 in 100 organisations have job-sharing, home working, or school term deals with only a quarter offering some optional part-time working and/or flexitime and only 18% allowing job-sharing.'

Some women managers pay out as much each month on childcare as their net monthly wage! They only continue to work because they derive tremendous job satisfaction from working and they do not wish to jeopardise their careers.

Support?

Where partners hold similar levels of managerial position it is invariably the woman who organises children, shopping, cleaning, washing, cooking and holidays in addition to her full-time job. That is not to say she receives no help from her partner, merely that it is often just that – help.

One way which works for some couples is for the working woman's partner to accept that hers is the major career and to remain content to support her and their home and family life. The woman in such partner-ships is under less stress and can let go of her feelings of guilt, knowing that her partner is coping at home. As long as this suits them both, this role reversal can prove very fruitful.

So much for the woman manager who chooses to share her life with a partner. What about those who remain single? Whilst there are benefits to having no partner, as we have already seen, there are also costs to be paid. If a woman chooses to remain single and forgo the pleasures, or otherwise, of a partner and/or children, she may suffer from recurring bouts of loneliness. Just having someone to talk with or sit quietly with in companionable silence can be therapeutic at the end of a long hard day at work.

There will be occasions when the woman manager who has chosen to remain on her own may find the lack of a partner a distinct disadvantage. Not only is there the loneliness of arriving home to an empty house, but here is also the feeling that maybe she is missing out in some way on things other women take for granted. If there are certain company functions she must attend, it can be very difficult without a partner, yet there is a need to be seen attending functions in order to continue on track in her career. Neither will it do to be seen turning up with a different partner on each occasion – that immediately labels you!

What a woman manager needs, if single, is a good friend she can turn to who understands some of the pressures she is under. It is often difficult to discuss problems of work or personal problems with a colleague. In most cases there are not enough women in similar positions to talk to. Discussing problems with subordinates can be difficult as it may be seen as a sign of weakness.

A natural follow on is stress, yet another cost to women managers. It has been argued persuasively that women managers face far more stress than men in similar circumstances. This is, at least in part, undoubtedly due to the additional pressures on women outside work as they attempt to balance all their commitments.

To Double-Clean?

A monetary cost, whether a partner is involved or not, is that of cleaning. Many women managers employ a cleaner to look after the house. Even those who remain single often employ a cleaner. It is difficult to motivate yourself to keep a home spick and span after a hard day at work. However, whether it always lowers the work burden is doubtful. Most women, when asked, admit that they feel morally obliged to clean the house before the cleaner arrives! Ask yourself – does this apply to you?

Are we Sitting Comfortably?

What are the costs to our out-of-work activities? Can a woman manager also manage a life that includes them? Unfortunately, they are often the first things to be dropped when the going gets tough. Yet women, as much as men, benefit if they take time to relax after the pressures of work. Many male managers feel they can stop off for a drink with colleagues after work before going home whilst most women would not even con-sider this as an option for all kinds of reasons. Most women would not dream of going for a drink on their own after work. It is still not considered 'the done thing.'

A woman invariably feels that she must get home to

clean, get a meal, see to the children and maybe finish off any work she takes home with her. Much of the responsibility for running the home falls on her. She is often the Chief Executive of the family.

Being single does not absolve a woman of her family responsibilities. There are usually parents to consider, as well as other close relatives. If she is an only child, or has brothers rather than sisters, it is she who is usually expected to take the responsibility for her parents in their old age. This adds to her responsibilities and gives little time for relaxation.

It can be difficult for most women managers to find the time for regular relaxation and it is far easier to stay at home and catch up on work. Too often schedules may be disrupted by meetings that overrun or visits away from home. We are not just talking about exercising, but enjoying the cinema, theatre, concerts, the company of others at various clubs or even a simple night out with friends. Often our work is at the cost of all these things. Maybe the time has come to get things in perspective and look at the benefits to be gained by taking a little more relaxation.

A leading member of Soroptomists International, a club set up for business women, has spoken recently of the difficulties in attracting working women managers. 'They have neither the time nor the inclination to join,' she said, 'yet they will join pure business clubs where they continue to talk of nothing but work!'

Regardless of the costs we have mentioned, the major benefit is that of self-fulfilment and the knowledge of a job well done. There is tremendous satisfaction to be gained from having 'made it' and you are a happier, more satisfied person in your private life when you are fulfilled in your work.

There is also the opportunity to empower others and help aspiring women managers on their way. Women managers need more role models to follow. There are still too few women in positions where they can empower others.

Perhaps one of the most important benefits is the additional income. There may be times when monetary costs exceed income, especially where there are young children involved, but these times pass and then the benefits are more apparent. The family has a higher standard of living and, if you are single, the extras that make life more comfortable are more easily available. The importance of your income should not be under-estimated. It buys you time, freedom and control. For many women it is the feeling of security and independence that comes with responsibility at work and an income to call her own that is the main benefit.

Dealing with Guilt

Guilt feelings are something everyone experiences. Women appear to feel guilt more than men over even small things and this is one of the causes of the additional stress suffered by women. Anything that has had to be left undone due to work gives rise to feelings of guilt. At some time we have all said, 'I feel so guilty. If I wasn't at work I would have done that.'

Guilt feelings surface for a variety of reasons and may be connected with home and personal relationships or, with work and working relationships. At home the feelings of guilt arise the moment that something that should have been done or remembered has been missed—family birthdays, appointments, PTA meetings, trips out and evenings in. It may be as simple as forgetting to iron a shirt for the next day.

However many or few children we may have does not prevent us feeling guilty for leaving them on their own, or in someone's care whilst we are at work. We spoke earlier in the chapter about 'latch-key kids' and the feelings that description aroused. Now this particular phrase has been dropped to be substituted by 'granny dumping.' The latest news stories tell of elderly, infirm parents being 'dumped' at hospitals or in nursing homes. Women whose parents are in need of care are being made to feel guilty because they are pursuing their careers at 'the expense' of their parents.

The fact is that, for the most part, elderly relatives are better cared for due to the additional income within the family. The families often have a good and loving relationship because the carers are not having to give up a career in the process.

At work, a woman manager may feel guilt at not helping another woman obtain promotion, even though she may know the person concerned was not good enough. We need to realise that not every woman will be a capable manager. Guilt may be triggered by a deadline missed, by something going wrong, by someone being upset; however it is aroused, the stress level increases with feelings of guilt.

We really need to tell ourselves that feeling guilty does not help. Whatever has been missed, forgotten, left, has now gone and feeling guilty will do nothing to change the situation. We cannot ensure that everything will be perfect, we can just do our best.

Careers, Families and 'Real Life'. The Way It really Is?

How does a career fit in with a family and the 'real life' outside work? We have already seen that on occasions the fit is not too good. However, many women manage to successfully combine a family and career.

The very fact that you feel fulfilled at work means that there is less time or inclination to worry about insignificant hiccups at home. Often children enjoy their mother working. They appreciate their improved life-style and the 'quality time' their mother has with them. Partners can get as much pleasure from you doing well in your career as if it were them – although much depends on the type of partner as we have seen. Whilst the manual work involved in running a home may tend be left, personal relationships will often gain a new dimension, with conversation and experiences no longer confined to the home.

We should not underestimate the difficulties of balancing a career and a family, however. We have already seen that this is the cause of additional stress to the woman manager. Sometimes it is difficult to separate ourselves into two different people. The composed, confident, well-briefed executive is often seen as being a completely different woman at home. It can be almost like being two different people.

Research into work/family conflicts experienced by female managers indicated that work/family conflict is more likely to be intensified by increased work demands than increased family demands. The highest level of work/family conflict was experienced by women managers who had a high level of family role importance and long work hours.

On reflection, this seems obvious yet it is so easy to stay at work to complete jobs, or not to take holidays that are owing. Have you ever said, 'I'm supposed to take the time off in lieu, but I never find the time?' If we are to obtain the right balance between family and career we must on occasions put the family first!

What about friends and long-standing relationships? Do these fall by the wayside as the career rises? We need to keep in touch with that 'real world' outside work. Too often it is very easy to cut off from anything unconnected with work or family. This can be even more pronounced for the single woman who does not have the restraining factor of the family. The temptation is to make work her life, especially if she has no close relatives. The problem comes when she retires or has to give work up. Then she has nothing.

When pursuing a career it is important not to be so single-minded that you cut yourself off from everything else. A woman engineer told us of how she single-mindedly set out to become the first female engineer to be sent abroad by her company. Unfortunately, in achieving her ambition she lost her partner who had decided he was 'superfluous to her requirements.'

Juggling Time

The one area of management that women managers need to be fully conversant with is time management.

Without exceptional time management skills, many women could not possibly manage to keep both home and career on line. The woman manager spends much of her life juggling time at work, at home and at play. Every minute is a constant trade-off. How many times have you traded doing one thing to make time for something else? Something on the lines of, 'I'll work until late tonight so I have time to take the children to school tomorrow.'

There may be times her partner needs her to be with him, or the children expect her to be there for them. Unfortunately these times very rarely fit in with work schedules and it becomes ever more difficult to fit everything in. How many times have you popped into the supermarket on your way home in the evening to buy food for that night? Thank goodness for late opening!

Today, our lives are dominated by time. We rush from meeting to meeting, place to place, taking telephone calls and issuing orders whenever we are in one place long enough. Is it any wonder that women managers suffer from stress? Not only are they balancing time at work, they are also the chief balancing act at home too.

In September 1992, the European Society of Cardiology was told that women are increasingly at risk of heart disease because of the stress of having to run the home, look after children and go out to work.

Research into the home life of working women showed that, as well as holding down a full-time responsible position at work, they were expected cook, shop, clean, wash etc. once they returned home. Most women, the report concluded, have two full-time jobs with an occasional assistant – their partner. No wonder they become experts at time management! This constant juggling with time and the trade-offs which are essential to the woman manager are one of the reasons for her taking so little 'time-out.' The time just is not there.

Letting Go

There are times when we have to let go. We all need time away from the pressures of work just as much as our male counterparts. The problem for women managers is that they do not just have pressure at work. When they are at home, there can be pressure from partners, children, relatives and friends.

Women can be poor delegators, especially at home. The feeling of 'if you want it done properly do it yourself' or 'it's quicker to do it myself than explain how to do it to someone else.' We have spoken of how we feel obliged to clean up before the cleaner arrives! Often it is the female partner who gets the children up, dressed, off to school, checks on elderly relatives and then dashes off to work. Shopping is carried out during a few spare moments at lunchtime or on the way home. She will not let go! This unwillingness to let go does not just apply at home. Women managers will often stay late at work to complete jobs and will then take work home to ensure they stay on top of the work load.

Eventually the woman manager needs to set some time aside to 'do her own thing,' be it a drink after work, an hour at a health club or merely a half-hour walk at lunchtime. Unless some time is set aside from the everyday pressures of life, there is a risk of stress building up. We need time to stand back and look at what is going on in our lives to enable us to take charge and direct our life.

Even at home there is a need to let go. If a woman chooses to spend some of her hard-earned money on employing a cleaner, sending her children to nursery and eating out rather than cooking after work, she should not feel guilt over it. The money is there to spend as you will and if spending it in this way makes life easier for you – fine. There is no need to feel that you should do everything yourself. Instead, tell yourself you are lowering the unemployment figures. This is the freedom and control that your own income gives you.

Research has shown that women managers find it difficult to let go. They feel that they have to keep going to complete tasks in case it is suggested things have been left due to family commitments. Sometimes letting go may be no more than an evening in with a friend. Talking problems over, sharing difficulties, laughing at each other's mistakes is one way of relaxing. Too often we even feel guilty at taking an evening away from the family and work! Remember, a problem shared is a problem halved.

Hints and Tips

- you cannot do everything. When things get too much, drop those jobs that cause you the most hassle
- leave some time for yourself each day, even if it is only half an hour. You need it

- try not to feel guilty when things are missed or forgotten
- practice good time management
- you are not responsible for everything – whatever anyone else may think!
- force yourself to delegate tasks to others
- keep in touch with your friends, however high you may climb. One day you will be glad of them.

Notes

1. Autrey, J. A., *Love and Profit: The Art of Caring Leadership*, Chapman, London, 1991, p. 202.
2. Stoner, C. R., and Hartman, R. I., 'Family Responsibilities and Career Progress' in *Business Horizons Journal*,Vol. 33, Issue 3, May/June 1990, pp.7–14.
3. Coe, T., *The Key to the Men's Club: Opening the doors to women in management*, Institute of Management Research Report, 1992.
4. Burden, H., 'The Case of the Disappearing Women', *Cosmopolitan*, September, 1992.
5. Institute of Manpower Studies, *Good Practice in the Employment of Women Returners*, University of Sussex, IMS, 1990.
6. Davidson, M. J., and Cooper, C. L., *Shattering the Glass Ceiling: The Woman Manager*, Chapman, London, 1992, p.6.

7

The Next Step –
How to Take It

> 'She who gets hired
> is not necessarily the one
> who can do that job best,
> but the one who knows
> the most about
> how to get hired.'
>
> Natasha Josefowitz

Is this the job for me? Is this the right time? In looking at any new job or any promotion opportunity, the starting point has to be with yourself. You need to identify the reasons why you are considering this change to your working life. Are you applying for a similar job at a higher level because you feel you are ready for this, or are you changing your career direction? Perhaps you are returning to work after a break, or anxious to leave a job where you are unhappy or undervalued. These various reasons for applying are very important because each separate reason brings with it a particular mental set. These will vary from feeling confident (I'm already doing a good job here so I must be in line for that promotion!) to concern about whether you will be seen as experienced enough for the new job.

More dramatically, you may feel that your life needs changes in all sorts of ways and be unsure about whether a career change will bring this about. A career move or promotion may bring about changes that you might not want, in relation to a new location or heavier time commitments. Sometimes it feels appropriate, although risky, to use your freedom to apply for a new job as an attempt to sort out personal issues which are far less tangible. At others times this may just compound the issues and make you lose sight of your professional capabilities.

Whatever your reasons, and they may be more than one, you need to be as clear as you can and think and talk them through with a close friend or mentor before you get down to the very serious business of applying. Do not apply if you are not serious as at a senior level, and as a woman you will be very visible and a less than serious application or too many withdrawals can be bad news. Do not expect miracles, either, although you can use a new job as a kick start to a new life.

Why Am I Applying?

Having some idea of how this opportunity fits into the pattern of your life and work, it is time to do the kind of self-awareness analysis that we have been urging throughout this book. What are the strengths you bring and what are the new opportunities for you in this situation? Which are the areas in which you are not yet competent and where are the threats and anxieties? You need to take a hard look, again, if possible with a mentor, and begin to list these qualities and concerns.

In this way you begin to identify your own sense of achievement and establish or review your personal career agenda for the future. It is also during this exercise that you become aware of any obstacles or areas where you need to develop more expertise or contacts. It is worth trying to visualise yourself actually doing the new job; take a quiet time and close your eyes to do this. It is an exercise which is worth the time and effort.

OK, I Want a New Job!

You have decided that it is time for you to move on or up and you want to take the next step. You will, of course, look in your own professional papers for adverts and will send for further particulars of a whole range of these to get a feeling for the scene. You should also look wider; the divide between the public and private sectors is being eroded and you may well have strengths to take from one into the other. It is also at this time that you begin to talk to people about your intentions and try to learn through the grapevine and networks what is about to come up. Now you begin to see why the hours spent networking are worth the investment! As you pass on details of jobs you know about but are not interested in to other women, they will return the favour and your circle of knowledge widens. You need to let it be known widely that you are actively seeking a new position. In the process of looking at new, more senior jobs, you inevitably begin to articulate what your own job is about. What you do on a day-to-day basis may sound very different as you begin to analyse it in the light of a job application. It may even be that you realise that the job you have is, in many ways, better for you than the one you are looking at. In which case, it is probably a question of reviewing your priorities.

Now I've Got the Details and It Looks too Senior for Me!

Something you should know: if a job specification lists ten skills the candidate should have, men will apply if they have experience in at least two. Women will not apply unless they can demonstrate expertise in at least eight. So, the job may not be right for you and hopefully your preparation will tell you this. On the other hand, you are probably tying one hand behind your back and not recognising your abilities and potential. Rarely, unless it is a sideways move, does anyone have experience in the job they are applying for. This is particularly true in management.

If you decide, with a little help from your friends, that you are going for this job, then this is the time for some serious research. Find out about the company or institution, using its public documents which you can ask to see, like accounts, brochures and strategic plans.

At certain levels of management the appointment procedures are themselves managed by others. These consultancy firms will handle the whole process from advertisement through to interview and you will find yourself dealing with professionals who are not necessarily experts in your field. The process may include psychometric testing, which some researchers argue is gender biased, and will probably involve a series of interviews outside of the place where you are applying to work. You will need, in preparation, to have visited the company you might wish to work for and to have gained enough answers to your questions to be sure that this is a place and organisation you would feel comfortable working for. At the highest levels, jobs may not even be advertised, or will be advertised only after some possible candidates have been identified. This process, unfortunately named 'head hunting,' may involve the consultants approaching key individuals who may not even have thought of applying. If you can, get yourself on to the lists of head hunting firms. They are keen to identify good people because this makes their job easier. However, it is important to realise that this process is, of itself, a new phenomenon and may, until women make and use the contacts, prove yet another obstacle to women's long march to the top. Networking and the use of mentors have to be the answer!

Filling in the Form

It is common practice for most firms to request the filling in of an application form as well as a letter in support of that application. This is the first thing to get absolutely right and it takes a great deal of time and care. You would be surprised at the number of applications made for quite senior posts in poor handwriting, with grammatical errors and an illegible photostat of an outdated CV. The message is quite clear to the employer: the candidate is not taking this job seriously and this firm is one on a list of many for someone seeking a job anywhere. So get your form and letter and CV typed. Agencies will do this if confidentiality is an issue at work. It is essential to read and check the completed documents before sending them off for accuracy of dates and information and for the overall 'look' of the finished products. At this point, in reading through, it is useful to make sure that your application form is focused on applying for this particular post and is not merely a record of what you are doing now. Before sending this off, ask a close friend or mentor to look at it and offer comments. Every application made, like every interview experienced, is part of our learning process, and it is possible, if you are either successful or unsuccessful, to look through each stage and see what you got right or wrong. Remember that if you were doing this as part of an expensive management training course, you would work hard at it. Use this as a free management development opportunity!

Preparing for the Interview

We have suggested previously the importance of researching the job and of thinking through the implications for you. We have stressed that every application is a learning process. This is also true for the interview itself. An interview may feel like a test and you may feel that you, as a person, are being judged and accepted or rejected, but this really is not the case. Each interview is a two way process and what is at stake both for you and the potential employer is the need to discover whether you and the job are really right for each other. Every appointment, especially in a difficult financial climate, represents a serious investment by the employer, of time and money. You have to be able to do the job, want to do it and be able to show your potential for development. All this has to come across in half an hour or so! Hence preparing exactly what you want to communicate is vital. Talk it through and try your ideas out on a friend or mentor.

A Checklist

- know the organisation
- understand what the job is about
- know what you want and where you want to go
- be clear that this job will help you on your career path
- have a vision of yourself in the job
- plan how you will convince an employer it is you they need
- work out what you will wear to the interview!

What Shall I Wear?

However well prepared you are, there are some practical issues which still need your attention. You have to make sure that you arrive in plenty of time and that your appearance sends the right signals for this job. This is not an easy issue, since you will still want to retain your individual style and, since there are fewer dress codes for women to help in this situation, you must give this careful thought. A suit is becoming much more the norm, even at interviews for more junior jobs. By dressing appropriately, in a way that fits the company image and the level of the job or that of the one above it, you are demonstrating that you understand the rules. You may later adapt or change these, but that is a different matter! Darker clothes are read as being more mature and more serious and extremes of accessories or any kind of distracting 'clutter' indicates, rightly or wrongly, an equivalent state of mind.

You need to feel comfortable and to wear clothes that fit the situations the interview process demands. For example, if you are taken on a tour of the premises, you do not need new shoes that make you hobble, tight skirts you cannot climb stairs in or a handbag that weighs you down. You are on display and a tour and informal meetings with staff can be as critical as the formal interview. Increasingly, the interview panel will receive comments from individuals and groups who have met the candidate, so you must look and sound right. The same goes for the lunch or pre-interview dinner; as with any business appointment, you are still on show and still at work. You may be the only female candidate and this alone will make you very visible and self-aware. Keep to the rules, listen a lot and make your uniqueness work for you. Having given all the warnings, it is also true that you can use this situation to your advantage. Women often relate well in social and small group situations, can be good listeners and observers and will certainly not go un-noticed.

The Day Dawns. . .

The day has arrived and so have you, well prepared, looking and feeling good (well, tell yourself that whatever!) and in control of the situation and yourself. Think positive, remember the visualisation you did of yourself actually doing this job and think how lucky the panel are to meet you. You are also interviewing them and making your mind up whether you want to invest your time and talent here. Do not be grateful, you have earned this, but do be aware that members of the panel are all individuals with their own worries and agendas and prejudices. Try to make the interview session something you and they enjoy, whatever the outcome. If not for this job, then you may impress them as suitable for something in the future. The individuals who interview you may themselves come from another company or department and may move on and you may well meet up again one day.

While waiting outside the interview room chat, if you can, to the secretary and certainly never ignore the possible force of her comments on you and how you treated her. Talk with other candidates, but do not be drawn into competitive banter, catch their panic or be intimidated by their apparent knowledge and confidence. There is always one candidate who knows the boss, the company and believes that because he is at the interview he has been given the job already. Make sure you keep yourself calm; go to the Ladies if you need to get away from a conversation which is disturbing you. Deep breaths and cold water on your wrists can help more than you think.

Dorothy Sarnoff has developed what she calls the 'Sarnoff Squeeze.' This involves leaning and pushing hard against a wall in a lunging position . She claims that it has miraculous results if you also combine the movement with letting out breath in a hiss. It is worth trying the exercise; many people swear by it. We would recommend, however, that you find a private place! Some stress is essential and provides positive energy and a sense of excitement. This is a new challenge, enjoy it.

Please Step this Way . . .

You enter the room confidently and, if you feel it appropriate, shake hands with the panel. Make eye contact with each individual and remember to do this throughout. It is really important at this stage to listen carefully and be sensitive to the mood of the group. The room setting and the chair's introduction will set the scene and give you some clues about the degree of formality expected. However relaxed and informal the panel seems, never drop your guard completely, they are interviewing you, for this short time, and you must give them your full attention and make them feel you understand what is expected and can handle it. It is at this stage also that you will pick up more clues about the job and the ways in which people interact within the company. Be alert and pick up any concerns or queries, albeit tactfully, before the interview ends.

Most interviews start with a 'warm-up' question to put you at your ease, but these are crucial moments. Research suggests that decisions are often made in the first few moments and based on the seeming trivia of appearance and manner of self-presentation. Occasionally, you will be unable to get it right and that may well be nothing to do with you, but with a whole set of pre-determined and unarticulated ideas held by the panel members. Luckily there is normally more than one person interviewing you and more often than not you can, by impressing the team with your preparedness and perceptive discussion, turn those prejudices round.

Likely Questions

- what are your strengths and weaknesses?
- where do you see yourself in five years time?
- why should we employ you rather than anyone else?
- why have you applied for this job?
- why are you leaving your current job?
- what do these 'gaps' in your CV mean? Were you away from the workplace then ?
- this job means a relocation, how do you feel about that?
- this job involves unsociable hours; how would you cope?

Some of these, you will notice, are new ways, within the law, of asking about your domestic situation. You need to persuade the panel, not necessarily by going into any personal details, that you have thought it through and can cope. Whilst on the one hand this is 'your business', it is vital to the employer to be reassured that you have already thought of these issues before applying for the post. The tone in which these questions are asked can vary and you may feel that the spotlight is on you in these matters because you are a woman. Until the game has changed and the presence of women is no longer unusual but the norm, we will have to negotiate a difficult path and learn to keep our integrity without looking as if we are unduly 'touchy' or unprepared for responsibility. It may help to point to your current work record and demonstrate with a practical example that you are committed and as flexible as the job requires you to be.

Be aware of the timing, you will normally be told how long it will last, and respond to the chair's attempts to bring things to a conclusion. Ask your questions if you have them and leave on a positive note, thanking them for their time and saying, if it is true, that you are as enthusiastic now as you were when you first submitted your application. If you are no longer 'a serious candidate' for the post, say so now and with tact.

What now?

If you get the job, the fun really begins and that is the subject of another book. If you don't, then you should ring the company and ask for feedback on why they did not see you as suitable. A good company may invite you to do this, through the Personnel section or the chair's PA and will spend time with you, on the phone or even in person, talking through your application. Keep an open mind; it may be that you and the job were not a marriage made in heaven, but it may be that you could have sold yourself more strongly or in a more appropriate manner. It is most important, at this stage, to recall that you have had a management training experience that would cost a great deal if you had to pay for it on a private training course. Do all of this quickly, as soon as you can after the interview, clarify what you have learnt and prepare to move on. It might also be useful to discuss this with your mentor and to seek guidance on those areas where you feel you need to work.

On the Other Side of the Desk. . .

We have spent a lot of time talking about being interviewed, but it is becoming increasingly the case at most levels within companies and institutions, that at least one woman is invited onto the interview panel. Your own post may well include interviewing as part of its requirements. Some would say that women approach the whole matter with a different set of experiences and expectations, and certainly many of the skills required in interview situations are those which we have already identified as women's areas of strength.

How far you can influence the form and content of the interview, so that it offers all candidates a fair chance and yet still encourages individuality to shine through, will depend on your position and on you. As chair, you can change things a lot. You can break the old patterns and interview in new ways, both in the way you physically organise the circumstances of the interview and in the management of the process. There are clear guidelines of good practice and these include person as well as job specifications. Training is available and all interview panel members should be encouraged to undertake this.

In interviewing, you have the opportunity to learn and to appraise and think through the whole process in relation to the matching of an individual to a company.

Does in fact the interview process itself represent the best means of assessing this? This is not a flippant question. The consequence of this interview could mean the tying up of both resources and other possibilities for the future of the company. The 'wrong' appointment can cost dearly. It might be that this is the moment, prior to interview, that you meet with the other interviewees and begin to form a very clear vision of what you are actually looking to gain from this employee.

- what kind of person are we looking for?
- how long can we reasonably expect them to stay in this post?
- what can we offer them after this?
- are we prepared to take a risk?
- who does this person need to get on well with, and at what level?
- what qualifications are essential, and which desirable?
- just how important to us is relevant experience?
- how seriously do we take the comments of referees?

Once the criteria have been established, you need to be clear that your role as a member of the interview panel gives you the right, within these guidelines, to ask questions of candidates and to offer your honest opinions in the discussion. This is not easy, especially if you are a 'token' or more junior woman on the panel. It is crucial to remember, however, that you are there to do a job and that even if your views differ from those of the others, if you handle the situation professionally, you will be respected. Do not be intimidated, ask for clarification and argue if you think that injustice is being done.

Interviewing, like being interviewed, is hard work and a learning experience. Each interview and each candidate is different and as an interviewee you need to sum up the culture of the company, so as an interviewer you will communicate that culture to candidates and others on the panel. You need to stay alert, be courteous and fair and to give off an air of calmness and control, To attract good people, you have to communicate to them that this is a good place to work with a management that offers leadership and direction.

Whichever side of the desk you sit, the chances are that you will change sides more than once in your career, so try to learn to welcome the challenge of interviews rather than dread them.

Conclusion

What we have been talking about throughout this book is power, both personal and professional. Like ambition, power is a word women sometimes shy away from, yet it is critical to our success. We need to define our own needs and be clear how, as managers, we are going to empower others. In the worlds in which we work, power sometimes has a connotation of force and it is treated as if it were finite. What women can do is to begin to explore the range of possibilities open to them, not only of ways of gaining power but, in gaining it, to use it to help others, demonstrating en route that empowering others is an effective and successful way of managing.

As with other areas explored within this book, we would suggest that each individual has to start with her own feelings. Working through, in this case, how she feels about power itself. One of the easiest things in all our professional lives is to criticise those with power as wrong-headed and perhaps wrong-hearted. Much more difficult is to construct the different ways in which power itself can be managed. This has to be the case if management is about getting things done and about having a vision for the future. Nothing can be achieved or gained from a position of powerlessness, and managers, who are leaders by definition, need to be able to understand how we can harness power to everyone's advantage.

On the other hand, as we have suggested, power is not a finite thing in itself. It has much to do with status and role, but also with the perception of others and ourselves. To be called 'a powerful woman manager' might invoke a positive image of someone who not only knows her own mind but is seen as such by others. From an early age women are taught that being powerful is the opposite of being passive. They learn that in men power appears as a legitimate strength but that in women it is less than 'feminine.'

Think, for instance, of the many nursery rhymes and fairy tales of our childhood where the active, powerful prince saves the passive or entrapped princess. Not one of these early tales demonstrates the ability of a female character to be powerful in her own right, through her own endeavours and achievements. As we grow up we begin to question these assumptions, but the essence of the story remains with us. One result is that we are taught to fear taking control and admitting to our own wants and desires. If we do this what will happen? Will we be judged 'different' or 'difficult'? If we assert ourselves, does this make us selfish? Does it mean that if we want and gain power, other people will no longer like us? People with power are viewed as different: sometimes viewed with envy, sometimes with scorn. We are surrounded by personal and professional dilemmas about power.

Power is not an abstract; if you are a manager, or aspiring to be a manager, your power will fall into different categories. You may have the power to hire and to fire; to make policy and to control finances. Each comes with its own set of responsibilities, to individuals and to the company. In the 1990s companies are aware of the need to 'invest in people' and perhaps this is a new way in which we can see power; power given to and used on behalf of others. This is power which is given away, facilitating the progress of others. The process of empowerment is critical to a lot of new thinking about management theory.

The notion of empowerment raises a whole new way of seeing managers, management and leadership skills. It is no longer seen as reasonable behaviour for a manager to give dictatorial orders to others and expect these to be carried out and be seen as the model for organisational relationships. The image of the woman as 'she who must be obeyed' is as anachronistic as the concept of 'petticoat tyranny.' A good leader wants to have the reassurance that others in her team are using to the full their potential and skills for their own professional development and satisfaction, but also for the benefit of the company. The ability and skill to empower others is now perceived as one of the most successful and effective ways to manage.

There are some problems peculiar to the woman manager. If as a manager your aim is to help others, you must be prepared to be seen by some people as weak. You might be seen as spending too much time worrying about individuals and their development rather than focusing on the tasks which have priority within the company. Since we are seen as 'natural carers' we need to face up to the way in which our very proper management style will be read. Otherwise our desire to empower others will be seen as 'favouritism' (especially if you are working to empower other women, or merely written off as being part and parcel of being a 'people person', 'oh, she's ever so kind but' . . .). We need to be clear about what we are doing, and why, and be sure to communicate our aims.

Do You Want to be Liked?

It is absolutely essential for all of us to work through our own feelings about power and management and to identify, where we can, our desires and motives as well as being conscious about our conditioning. Part of becoming a manager is the process of adjustment to a position as being perceived as 'not being one of the gang', perhaps being the lone woman at the top and subsequently isolated within the workplace. Coupled with this has to be a certain degree of acceptance that through your position, your power, your responsibility and your salary others might not see you in quite the same light as you see yourself! So one of the first questions to be asked is, 'how much do I need to be liked at work?' The further up the professional ladder you go, the more your behaviour language will progressively separate you.

How important is it for you to be universally liked? Do you find yourself 'housekeeping' at work, either by making the coffee, keeping the peace or working on all those maintenance jobs that need doing but get left undone? This role may feel satisfying and it is pretty sure to feel familiar, but is it what you want, does it give you a chance to show the heights you are capable of rising to; does it empower you? Facing up to a mix of feelings may be revealing. How do you actually feel about the roles you play or are expected to play as 'carer'?

- resigned! I'm used to doing this at home trying to keep everyone happy!
- frustrated! Half my time at work is spent propping up other people rather than being able to get on with what I want and need to do
- resentful! why me? It's not fair – no-one else does all this, no-one ever does this for me!
- invisible! After all I have done here no-one even noticed at that meeting
- hurt! It's not that I mind doing all of this as well as the job, but I can't understand why I'm not taken seriously . . . having needs, ambitions and talents too
- comfortable!

Many of these reactions may sound familiar. Just like Cinderella in the story, we in the workplace, whilst making endless cups of coffee, listening to our colleagues moaning, tidying up, are in danger of waiting for our prince to come and to get recognition for all the things we do. But fairy tales are just that; no prince really arrives and no-one notices you for your talents and skills used behind the scenes and in secret. No-one gets promoted simply for being nice! Make sure your talents are noticed and not exploited.

The barriers to achieving our own power and potential are not all internal and the result of socialisation. There are prejudices and people do construct stereotypes. The recruitment and employment practices of some organisations remain discriminatory, to women and others. It is in such situations that we feel most frustrated and powerless and it is at these times that our goals need to be most clear in our minds. If you are stuck, in a particular job or at a particular level, then it is even more crucial for you to have a sense of your own power and the options open to you. You can leave and move on, or you can expand your horizons, do your job in a new way, negotiate a new set of responsibilities or undertake training.

You can always network and share your concerns with others. At the bottom line, however, you must grasp the nettle and decide what you want and how to get it. Prince Charmings are rare enough, goodness knows, and those bearing an offer of a top job just cannot be relied upon to turn up and rescue you.

It is necessary to set goals and to plan. Your goals will reflect your strengths and your potential, given new opportunities or training. They will change; at each stage you will review them and probably set yourself harder tasks. To achieve your goals you may have to take risks and venture into the unknown. The frustration of staying with what is safe and known out of fear is something all of us can recognise and it can be stifling. Many women in the 90s are setting up alone in small businesses, acting as consultants and trainers, or writing. They will have identified their ability to live with risk and the empowerment they feel from being their own boss. Others of us can achieve more within larger organisations and need that financial security and community of co-workers in order to stimulate and fulfil us.

Plan for the future, be aware of what you can do, or could do with training or the chance to prove yourself and hang on to that vision. Most of all, let others know what you are aspiring to. If Prince Charming has gone missing so has his handsome peer who woke Sleeping Beauty from her slumbers. Most of us have waited and hoped and most of us have learnt that results will not happen unless we work for them. If you can not find your answer where you are, then do something about it.

You can be known for doing your job well; that is a base line, especially for women. You can be recognised as someone with ideas, but only if you communicate these publicly so that your name is attached to them. It is good to be known for something in particular, that is a 'cause' of your own and with which you are associated. Keep visualising yourself at the top, or wherever you want to be and persuade others by the way you dress, behave and speak that you are already almost there. Confidence is the key and it is elusive. Women are taught to question and demur; modesty is one of our traditional virtues. Giving credit to others is powerful; denying credit to yourself, when it is deserved, is of no use to anyone.

As a group of women, we can only offer such firm advice because we know it is what we need to hear ourselves. We know we are good, as you know you are good, but sometimes we all forget and feel invisible in the places where we work and where we spend so much of our time. There are many areas we have not covered in this book. You might want to find out about psychometric testing, for example, or how to speak in public. Your perspective on our comments will depend on where you stand in your company, what level you are at and where you want to be. You may work in an area of traditional female appointments, like health or education and find that your glass ceiling is at middle management level. You may work in an area where women are fewer, like technology or the sciences and you will face another set of issues. What we hope, however, is that there is enough here from our common experience to help you understand where you are and take control of some of the work situations you face. We are still struggling and if you have comments or further hints and tips, we would like to hear from you.

The story of every woman manager has no end; as each woman begins a new chapter and moves through her own glass ceiling the story goes on. To be continued. . .

Bibliography

Archer, J., and Lloyd, B., *Sex and Gender*, Penguin, Harmondsworth, 1982.

Autry, J., *Love and Profit: The Art of Caring Leadership*, Chapmans, London, 1991.

Boydell, T., and Hammond, V. (eds.), 'Men and Women in Organisations', *Management Education and Development*, Vol. 16, No. 2, 1985.

Bryce, L., *The Influential Woman: How to Achieve Success Without Losing Your Femininity*, Piatkus, London, 1989.

Chernesky, R., and Bombyk, M., 'Woman's Ways and Effective Management', *Affilia*, Vol. 3, No. 1, Spring 1988.

Clutterbuck, D. and Devine, M. (eds.), *Businesswomen: Present and Future*, Macmillan, London, 1987.

Coe, T., *The Key to the Men's Club: Opening the doors to women in management*, Institute of Management Research Report, 1992.

Cooper, C., and Davidson, M., *High Pressures: Working Lives of Women Managers*, Fontana Paperbacks, London, 1989.

Coyle, A., and Skinner, J., *Women and Work: Positive Action for Change*, Macmillan Education, London, 1989.

Davies, P., *Status: What it is and How to Achieve it*, Piatkus, London, 1991.

Davidson, M., and Cooper, C., *Stress and the Woman Manager*, Martin Robertson, Oxford, 1983.

Faludi, S., *Backlash: The Undeclared War Against Women*, Chatto and Windus, London,1992.

Faux, S., *Wardrobe*, Piatkus, London, 1988.

Firth-Cozens, J., and West, M., *Women at Work*, Open University Press, Milton Keynes,1991.

Gray, H. L., 'Gender considerations in school management: masculine and feminine leadership styles', in Riches, C., and Morgan, C. (eds.) *Human Resource Management in Education*, The Open University Press, Milton Keynes,1989.

Handy, C., *The Age of Unreason*, Hutchinson, London, 1989.

The Report of the Hansard Society, *Women at the Top*, London, 1990.

Harriman, A., *Women/Men/Management*, Praeger, Eastbourne, 1985.

Hearn, J. et al., *The Sexuality of Organization*, Sage, London,1989.

Hennig, M., and Jardine, A., *The Managerial Woman*, Pan Books, London, 1979.

Hertz, L., *Business Amazons*, Methuen, London,1987.

Josefowitz, N., *Is This Where I Was Going?* Columbus, London, 1983.

Kanter, R. M., *When Giants Learn to Dance: Mastering the Challenges of Strategy Management and Careers in the 1990's*, Unwin Paperbacks, London, 1990.

Leary, M., 'Men and Women; what are the differences and does it matter?', *Management Education and Development*, Vol. 16, No. 2, 1985.

Loden, M., *Feminine leadership, or How to succeed in Business without being one of the Boys*, Times Books, New York, 1985.

McLoughlin, J., *Up and Running: Women in Business*, Virago, London, 1992.

Mcdonald, J., *Climbing the Ladder: How to be a Woman Manager*, Methuen-Mandarin, London,1989.

Metcalf, A., and Humphries, M. (eds.) *The Sexuality of Men*, Pluto Press, London, 1985.

Miles, R., *Danger, Men at Work*, Futura, London, 1983.

Nicolson, N., and West, M., *Managerial Job Change: Men and Women in Transition*, Cambridge University Press, Cambridge, 1988.

Richards, C., and Morgan, C., *Human Resource Management In Education*, Open University Press, Milton Keynes, 1989.

Roddick, A., *Body and Soul*, Edbury Press, London, 1991

Rothwell, S., 'Is Management a Masculine Role?', *Management Education and Development*, Vol. 16, Pt. 2, 1985.

Segerman-Peck, L. M., *Networking and Mentoring: A Woman's Guide*, Piatkus, London,1991.

Tannen, D., *You Just Don't Understand: Women and Men In Conversation*, Virago, London,1992.

Women's Organisations, Campaigns, Networks: Addresses

We have stressed throughout the book the need for women to network. Below are some useful addresses to help you in this process. We would like especially to refer you to the Professional Women's Development Network at Staffordshire University with which all the authors of this book are associated. One of us, Maureen Atkinson, runs the network, which offers training, seminars and a range of opportunities all over the country for aspirant women managers or would-be managers to get together and share experiences. PWDN can be contacted via:

Maureen Atkinson
PWDN
Centre for Enterprise and Innovation
Staffordshire Business School
Staffordshire University
Stafford ST18 OAD
Tel: 0785–52331

Belgravia Breakfast Club
c/o Sheraton Park Tower Hotel
101 Knightsbridge
London SW1X 7RN
Tel: 071–235–8050

City Women's Network
925 Uxbridge Road
Hillingdon Heath
Middlesex UB10 0NJ
Tel: 081- 569–2351

European Association of Professional Secretaries
(EAPS)
Barbara Smith, Secretary
Heathrow Business Centre
Terminal 2
Heathrow Airport
Hounslow
Middlesex TW6 1EU
Tel: 071–371–2443

European Network of Women (UK section)
Anne M. McGlone
52–54 Featherstone Street
London EC2V 8RT
Tel : 071–720–9382

European Women's Management Development
Network
c/o 27 Brewer Street
Brighton BN2 3HH
Tel: 0273 686652

National Alliance of Women's Organisations (NAWO)
279/281 Whitechapel Road
London E1 1BY
Tel: 071–247–7052

Network
9 Abbots Yard
35 King Street
Royston
Herts SG8 9AZ
Tel: 0763 242225

Through the Glass Ceiling
c/o Dr Vivienne Wylie
University of Wolverhampton
Tel: 0902- 323433

Townswomen's Guild
Chamber of Commerce House
75 Harborne Road
Birmingham B153DR
Tel: 021–456–3435

UK Federation of Professional and Business Women
23 Ansdell Street
Kensington
London W8 5BN
Tel: 071–938–1729

Women and Training
c/o CSA
15 Harwood Road
London SW6 4QP
Tel: 071–736–6975

Women In Banking
c/o Caroline Gaffney
National Westminster Bank
166 Camden High Street
London NW1 ONS
Tel: 071–485–7121

Women in BP
Britannia House,
Moor lane
Moorgate
London EC2 9BU
Tel: 071–920–3896

Women in Higher Education Network
King's College
Cambridge CB2 1ST
Tel: 0223–350411

Women in Information Technology
c/o IT Strategy Services
2 Eastbourne Avenue
London W3 6JN
Tel: 081–992–3575

Women in Management
64 Marryat Road
Wimbledon
London SW19 5BN
Tel: 081–748–1427

Women in Public Life
c/o 110 Riverview Gardens
London SW13 9RA
Tel: 081–748–1427

Women in Science and Engineering
Head of Centre
TICST
Trent University
Burton Street
Nottingham NG1 4BU
Tel: 0602 418418

Women's Engineering Society
c/o Eugenis Maxwell
Imperial College of Science and Technology
Department of Civil Engineering
Imperial College Road
London SW7 2BU
Tel: 071–589–5111 ext. 4731

300 Group
36–37 Charterhouse Square
London EC1M 6EA
Tel: 071–600–2390

300 Group Educational Trust
c/o 4 Slayleigh Avenue
Sheffield S10 3RB
Tel: 0742 304098

For further information refer to:
Directory of 150 Women's Organisations
Women's National Commission
Cabinet Office
Government Offices
Horse Guards Road
London SW1P 3AL
Tel: 071–270–590